Lillian Too
Jennifer Too

FORTUNE & FENG SHUI

DRAGON

2021

KONSEPBOOKS
ASTROLOGY . FENG SHUI . INSPIRATIONS

Fortune & Feng Shui 2021 Dragon

by *Lillian Too* and *Jennifer Too*
© 2021 Konsep Lagenda Sdn Bhd

Text © 2021 Lillian Too and Jennifer Too
Photographs and illustrations © Konsep Lagenda Sdn Bhd
Cover Art © Josh Yeo Zhu Lin

The moral right of the authors to be identified as authors of this book has been asserted.

Published by KONSEP LAGENDA SDN BHD (223 855)
Kuala Lumpur 59100 Malaysia

For more Konsep books, go to *www.lillian-too.com* or *www.wofs.com*
To report errors, please send a note to errors@konsepbooks.com
For general feedback, email feedback@konsepbooks.com

Notice of Rights

Notice of Liability

ISBN 978-967-329-297-4
Published in Malaysia, September 2020

DRAGON 2021

BIRTH YEAR	WESTERN CALENDAR DATES	AGE	KUA NUMBER MALES	KUA NUMBER FEMALES
Earth Dragon	23 Jan 1928 - 9 Feb 1929	93	9 East Group	6 West Group
Metal Dragon	8 Feb 1940 - 26 Jan 1941	81	6 West Group	9 East Group
Water Dragon	27 Jan 1952 - 13 Feb 1953	69	3 East Group	3 East Group
Wood Dragon	13 Feb 1964 - 1 Feb 1965	57	9 East Group	6 West Group
Fire Dragon	31 Jan 1976 - 17 Feb 1977	45	6 West Group	9 East Group
Earth Dragon	17 Feb 1988 - 5 Feb 1989	33	3 East Group	3 East Group
Metal Dragon	5 Feb 2000 - 23 Jan 2001	21	9 East Group	6 West Group
Water Dragon	23 Jan 2012 - 9 Feb 2013	9	6 West Group	9 East Group

Cover Art by Josh Yeo Zhu Lin
Features a magnificent celestial Dragon embodying all that is auspicious from the winds and the waters. In 2021, the Dragon enjoys incredible success potential.

CONTENTS

Chapter One

YEAR OF THE METAL OX   11

The Influence of the Elements   15

The 24 Mountains Chart of 2021   24

The Luck of Big & Small Auspicious   25

Luck from the Heavens   28

The General Star brings power & authority   29

Take Heed of the Star of Yin House   29

Protect against the Robbery Star   30

Yearly Conflict & Yearly Killings   31

Averting the Natural Disaster Star   33

Luck of the 12 Animal Signs   33

Wealth Luck in 2021   38

Love Luck in 2021   40

Study Luck in 2021   43

Health Luck in 2021   44

Chapter Two

ELEMENT LUCK OF THE DRAGON IN 2021   46
Much success potential to tap this year

Dragon's Element Luck Chart 2021   48

The 9 Year Old Water Dragon   55

The 21 Year Old Metal Dragon   56

The 33 Year Old Earth Dragon   59

The 45 Year Old Fire Dragon   61

The 57 Year Old Wood Dragon   63

The 69 Year Old Water Dragon   65

The 81 Year Old Metal Dragon   66

Chapter Three

FOUR PILLARS CHART 2021   69

A Year of Strong Water indicates strong competition   71
Balance of Yin & Yang   74
Clash of Sheep with Ox   75
Special Link between Ox and Rat   77
No Prosperity Luck... but hidden wealth!   79

Special Stars of 2021

Star of Prospects brings opportunities   85
Star of Powerful Mentors attracts benefactors   87
Aggressive Sword Star is a double-edged sword   89
Flower of Romance Star make marriages vulnerable   92

Chapter Four

FLYING STARS OF 2021   96

Heavenly Star rules the year   97
Enhance the center grid with the Dragon   99
Invoking power of the 8 Immortals   100
Enhance for Future Prosperity in the NE   105
Activate for Love & Romance in the East   108
Transform Five Yellow into Good Fortune in the SE   115
Victory Star brings Winning Luck to the South   116
Suppress the Quarrelsome Star in the SW   121

Enhance Prosperity Star 8 in the West 124

Beware Betrayal & Loss in the NW 130

Suppressing Illness in the North 134

Appease Tai Sui in the NE 137

Beware Three Killings in the East 139

Chapter Five
DRAGON INTERACTING WITH OTHER SIGNS 142
Dragon has to try harder when it comes to relationships

DRAGON/RAT - Challenging year. Supporting each other 154

DRAGON/OX - Difficult with two captains 156

DRAGON/TIGER - Different approaches lead to dissent 158

DRAGON/RABBIT - Passion and romance await these two! 160

DRAGON/DRAGON - Plenty of laughs but no true loyalty 162

DRAGON/SNAKE - Making a fabulous team in 2021 164

DRAGON/HORSE - Unlikely match blessed by the heavens 166

DRAGON/SHEEP - Uncomfortable relationship 168

DRAGON/MONKEY - A great deal of sympatico 170

DRAGON/ROOSTER - Rooster gives Dragon a leg up 172

DRAGON/DOG - Deep incompatibility worsens in 2021 174

DRAGON/BOAR - Neither great nor terrible together 176

Chapter Six
DRAGON'S MONTHLY HOROSCOPE FOR 2021 178
Big dreams and potential but needs better staying power

Feb 2021 - Starting the year well with friends 179

March 2021 - Quarrelsome chi makes you disagreeable 182

April 2021 - Feeling listless and lacking in energy 185

May 2021 - Victory Star brings new hope   188
June 2021 - Misfortune luck gets magnified beware   191
July 2021 - Strong luck brings joy & success   194
Aug 2021 - Robbery Star sours the energy   197
Sept 2021 - Luck falls from the heavens!   200
Oct 2021 - Sum-of-Ten but beware of Five Yellow   203
Nov 2021 - Relationhips matter   206
Dec 2021 - Arguments abound. Beware.   209
Jan 2022 - Illness Star impacts on energy levels   212

Introduction to the
Year 2021

Chapter 1

YEAR OF THE METAL OX

The coming year is the Year of the Metal Ox, a year when harvests are reaped as a result of old-fashioned hard work. It takes on the nature of the diligent Ox, whose finest qualities are its stability and steadfastness, the sign that symbolizes all the hard work that has to be done in order to prepare for the harvests and prosperity that follows. While the coming year can be prolific, there are few shortcuts to be had. Those who put in the hours and who match their effort with their wit will be those who reap the most from the year. This will not be a time for easy money or overnight speculative gains. It will be a year when substance wins out over panache, and when those who put emphasis on building solid foundations will prosper. One should strive to work first at what one can bring to the table, before making promises or trying to convince others of one's potential.

THE TOILING OX

This is the year of the Metal Ox, so it is one in which the Earth element of the Ox gets constantly exhausted by its heavenly stem of Metal. Earth produces Metal, so is exhausted by it. This is a year when the Ox has to constantly keep up its efforts to stay ahead. Individuals who are dedicated and disciplined will be the most effective and the most successful. The year can be an industrious one, but only if one acts industriously. There is good progress to be made for those who consciously and actively mirror the attributes of the steady Ox. It will be a year void of lightning speed success but conscientious work pays off. It is a year that rewards hard work over talent, where practice trumps winging it.

FORMIDABLE FRIENDS AND FOES

The Ox sign makes a loyal friend but also a formidable enemy, so the year will see both sides of this coin. Competitive pressures will be tough, but those with robust teams of collaborators and allies will succeed. Factions will form and there will be both poignant friendships and daunting foes. Those that stand alone will find it difficult to navigate through the various obstacles that the year offers up.

The Paht Chee of 2021 features both a troublesome clash and a promising alliance in its earthly branch line up. There is a clash between the Ox and the Sheep in the Day Pillar, but also an encouraging connection between the Ox and the Rat in the Hour Pillar. It is a year when friendships matter, so one must work at keeping one's friends. Those that slip the net to the other side could become intimidating enemies. People will tend to hold grudges and have long memories. The advice is to avoid offending the wrong people with careless words and unthinking actions. Skins are thin and offense is taken at the smallest acts of offhandedness.

THE LEADER REIGNS SUPREME

The twelve months from February 4th 2021 to February 4th 2022 will support people in leadership positions. Those who have recently risen to high office or who were promoted last year, whether in Government or in Commerce, will feel the benefits of the year's energies. Such individuals enjoy the buoyancy of the winds and waters that translate into a powerful flow of auspicious

PAHT CHEE CHART 2021			
HOUR	DAY	MONTH	YEAR
壬 Yang Water	癸 Yin Water	庚 Yang Metal	辛 Yin Metal
壬 子 Yang Water Rat	己 未 Yin Earth Sheep	甲 寅 Yang Wood Tiger	己 丑 Yin Earth Ox

heaven luck. They benefit from a special vitality that aids their decision-making. Their actions carry weight and they find it easy to garner support for what they want to do.

With the #6 Heaven Star taking center stage in the year's Flying Star chart, leaders and those in positions of power are blessed with the mantle of heaven. It instills in them great authority and effect over their charges so they will have greater ability to influence the outcome of what they are engaged in.

This year favours leaders, chiefs, bosses, managers and directors of all kinds, and in all fields.

The danger this year is that the #7 afflictive star has arrived in the NW, the sector that represents the Patriarch. With leaders so powerful and with the treacherous #7 star in its home location, this brings the risk that those in power may use their position for harm rather than for good. Leaders with strong moral ethics can effect very positive change with a big and lasting impact, but those who act on a whim could end up making disastrous decisions that affect the fortunes of many.

The presence of the Ox-Sheep clash in the chart suggests that while leaders may be powerful within their own spheres, they meet with hostility from opposing interest groups, and leaders of other nations and organizations. Different blocs will have differing agendas, and when compromises cannot be reached, there will be conflict and struggle.

On the world stage, the influence of the #7 on the leader suggests there will be much fighting energy, and even risk of war. US-China trade relations will continue to deteriorate, with effects impacting more and more nations. Worrying alliances may be formed. There will be unified groups but it will not be one unified assembly; there will be powerful diverse groups that clash and clatter.

Conspiracy theorists may well have some premise to their conjectures; this becomes ever more likely if the ominous influence of the excessive Metal in the year's chart is not strongly suppressed. All may not be what it seems to be on the surface.

THE INFLUENCE OF THE ELEMENTS

METAL *represents authority*

METAL in 2021 stands for RESOURCES, but it also stands for AUTHORITY. Unfortunately, in 2021, authority may not always be benevolent. This year there is almost too much Metal energy, and too much makes the ominous side of this element stronger. Leaders become more powerful, and power here has to potential to corrupt. Checks and balances become more important, as the year could produce leaders who make unscrupulous decisions, taking into account only their own personal agendas.

This affliction affects not just leaders on the world stage but those in one's immediate sphere as well – bosses, community leaders, mentors, teachers, parents. If this Metal energy is not kept under control, it could lead to disastrous consequences in one's personal daily life. The effects of this can feel very real and close to home.

WHAT TO DO: We suggest displaying a **red-faced Kuan Kung**, the powerful Warrior God in the home and office to protect against the excess of Metal element energy. Having this God of War and God of Wealth in the home ensures you stay on the winning side of the element luck effect. Kuan Kung will ensure you make judicious decisions that end up benefiting you and your family in the long run. Gives you courage to move forward but tempers any misplaced bravado.

Red-faced Kuan Kung with 5 victory flags

2. Wearing jewellery in precious Metals fashioned as **sacred syllables** and **symbols** transforms the effect of Metal from autocratic to benevolent. It helps keep you protected from harm and ensures you do not lose the support of the people who matter most to your prospects in life- eg. Your boss, your parents, your teachers.

WATER *represents competition*
WATER in 2021 stands for FRIENDS and FOES, which are present in equal measure. Both have an equivalent part to play in the outcomes that follow. Because the year is one of STRONG WATER, the element of Water this year needs to be treated with caution. Too much of it could tip the scales over, attracting fierce rivalry and underhand tactics by one's competition, rather than cultivating strong allies that stay loyal.

This year it becomes especially important to carry protective amulets that guard against betrayal and disloyalty. Carrying an image of **Kuan Kung with Anti-Betrayal Amulet** will help protect against becoming a victim of these energies. Always give others suitable respect, and don't disregard the dangers of allies changing sides. If the incentive becomes attractive enough, they will. Don't take anything too personally if you can adopt the stoic outlook of the Ox where you make the most of the opportunities open to you without complaining too much what is fair or not fair. You can effectively buffer against many of the pitfalls of the year.

THE COLOR BLUE – Blacks and blues stand for Water energy. While water to the Chinese traditionally represents money, this year it also signifies competition. Using too much of this color this year holds the danger of fueling rivalry and competitiveness amongst one's peers. Do not don too much black, and when you do, try to add a splash of color to neutralize its more sinister effects. Place the **Celestial Water Dragon** in the home to keep this element under control.

FIRE *brings wealth*

FIRE in 2021 stands for WEALTH LUCK. This is the element that appears to be completely missing from the year's chart and thus is the one we must actively work at replacing. There is hidden wealth brought by the Tiger, but this needs a trigger for it to be actualized. We suggest wearing the color red in free abandon this year. Remember, this is the Year of the Ox, an Earth sign whose inner vitality gets spurred on by the wonderful energy of Fire.

THE COLOR RED - Red to the Chinese is always considered lucky. It is a color of celebration and carnival. It is traditionally used in all auspicious occasions, and as we move into the new year of 2021, it is especially important to wear plenty of red! For the first 15 days of the Lunar New Year, we recommend getting yourself a red outfit for each day. Keep up this ritual through the entire 15 days of celebrations to ensure its effects can get you through the year. This is an excellent way to "fuel up" for the year, as it is a year when the element of Fire is glaringly missing.

 In the home, keep the lights bright throughout the year. Change your lightbulbs whenever they start to flicker or lose energy, and don't try to save on the electricity bill by constantly turning off the lights! It is far more important to work at keeping this element properly energized through the year. Don't be penny wise and pound foolish. Lights represent Fire energy, and Fire energy represents wealth and prosperity in 2021.

NEW WEALTH WALLET: Each year it is an extremely lucky ritual to get yourself a new wallet and transfer some money from your old wallet over to your new one, while adding in some brand new notes (best if from cash received as a Chinese New Year ang pow, or from one's latest drawn salary or bonus). You can also keep the **Wealth God Sitting on a Tiger** in the form of a Gold Card inside your wallet; very

For Wealth

auspicious as the Tiger is the sign that brings hidden wealth to the year.

Each year we design a wallet to vibrate and sync with the energies of the year, and for 2021, our wealth wallet features the stock market bull. It is the Year of the Ox and the Wall Street Bull is a most auspicious symbolic cousin of the sign of the year. The Wall Street Bull represents your investments going up, and your asset wealth growing.

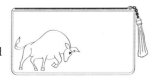

We also have the **Asset Wealth Bull** with wealth amulet which will attract wealth-generating luck to any home which invites it in. Display prominently in the West where the *Star of Current Prosperity* has flown to this year or on your desk in front of you where you work. The idea is to see it daily and its subliminal effects will magically influence your actions and ability to attract wealth luck into your life.

WOOD *brings growth*

WOOD is the element that stands for growth. In 2021, it also signifies intelligence and creativity. It is what brings fresh new ideas to the mix, encouraging a blossoming of imagination and ingenuity. As we foray further into the new decade, old ideas will increasingly lose appeal and old technologies become obsolete with increasing speed. These need to be replaced and they will, and it will be those who can dream up the new ideas, methods, designs and technologies that will profit.

For the individual looking at making it in a rapidly changing world, it will be enhanced creativity and thinking outside the box that will help you. Surround yourself with the vibrant energy of plants and greenery, invite fresh flowers displayed in auspicious vases into your living space. If you live in a modern skyscraper city where feasting on green is difficult or unusual, look for ways to introduce indoor gardens into your home and office space, take regular time to visit parks and gardens, or make time to visit the countryside to refuel and recharge your senses with the power of nature.

THE COLOR GREEN – Greens of all kinds represent innovation and vision in 2021. Fill your wardrobe with lots of this color in emerald green, lime green, neon green, shamrock, chartreuse, sage, seafoam… all of these will inject your wardrobe with a fresh dash of

inspiration and will attract wonderfully
inspired energies into your aura. Green
this year is very lucky and brings to the
wearer a new lease of life. If you have been
feeling dull, uninspired or at a crossroads
in life, introducing a pop of bright green into
what you wear or carry will give you the boost you
need to change track, get moving, get started. It is the
"energizing" colour of the year and should be made
use of liberally and profusely.

TEND YO YOUR GARDEN: There's nothing that
invokes better yang Wood energy than thriving plants
and greenery. Make a trip to your local nursery and
bring home some vibrant new plants to add to your
garden. If you live in an apartment, introduce some
live potted plants into your living space. This will stir
up the creative juices in you needed to dream up new
ideas and to hatch ingenious strategies for your work
and in your life.

EARTH *brings power & influence*
EARTH in the Year of the Ox is the
intrinsic element of the animal sign of
the year. It is the element that symbolizes
stability, strength and permanence. It is the element
that ensures that however crazy the energy gets,
however quickly the world changes around us, we
can dig our heels deep and stay grounded with
our values and our visions intact. Earth energy will

prevent us being light-eared and light-headed, or easily influenced. In 2021, the element of EARTH also signifies recognition and power. It brings the luck of rank and position, and boosts one's chances when it comes to promotion and upward mobility, whether in one's career or in any climb to the top of any organization. Earth energy brings you influence and command and will make people listen to you.

EARTH COLORS – Wearing shades of earth tones brings you respect and makes people listen to you. It keeps you rational and well-balanced and envelops you with an aura of dependability. An excellent color group to use when you need others to take you seriously. Earth colors include yellow, orange, beige and cream, in all their shades. Wear such colors when you feel you need others to take notice of you, when you want to boost your influence over others and when you need people to listen to you. Those of you ambitious for your career to get a boost will benefit greatly from making use of earth colors.

THE 24 MOUNTAINS CHART OF 2021

The compass wheel around which the animals are positioned contain 24 mountains, which attract different stars each year. The overall fortunes of the year get enhanced or disabled depending on which

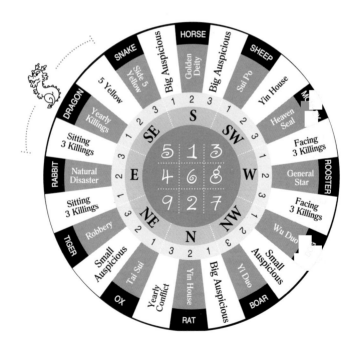

stars settle into which corners. Some years will have more auspicious stars, and some less, and their positions around the wheel impact on each animal sign differently.

THE LUCK OF BIG & SMALL AUSPICIOUS

One of the luckiest indications from this chart are the Big and Small Auspicious Stars, and in 2021, we have 5 of such stars making an appearance. The year enjoys three **Big Auspicious** stars and two **Small Auspicious** stars. The animal signs that benefit from these are the **Horse**, **Snake**, **Sheep**, **Rat**, **Boar**, the **Dog**, **Ox** and **Tiger**. The locations of these stars are spread out giving the above animal signs the potential to seize opportunities that come their way.

The sign that benefits most from this indication is the **HORSE**. The Horse enjoys two Big Auspicious stars, which suggests that after two difficult years, this sign is ready to take flight. The free-spirited Horse person can finally seize what it has been grappling after; this is a year when this sign can take risks and put wholehearted effort behind their passions. It is a year when the Horse should not rest on its laurels, because the big time has arrived.

The other signs enjoying Big Auspicious are the **Snake** and **Sheep**, and the **Rat** and **Boar**. These signs also have the potential to go after big dreams and, to

realize big ambitions they may have been harboring. For these signs, opportunities will be plentiful. Success comes for those who are hungry and resolute. Remember that this year, results do not come immediately, so one must not get discouraged if the path to actualization seems long or even impossible. The winners will be those with the staying power to keep at it and stay the course. Hold on to your dreams, and don't change your mind at every setback. Trust in your instincts and passions, and don't give power to those who disturb your mind or pour cold water on your ideas.

While the Stars of Big Auspicious bring really fabulous blessings, so do the Stars of Small Auspicious. These have the same effect as their big brother stars, but they bring success in smaller measures and in stages. The signs enjoying Small Auspicious this year are the **Ox**, **Tiger**, **Dog** and **Boar**. For these signs, they are likely

to meet with small successes that form the stepping stones to bigger success later on. For these signs, this is a year for building firm foundations and laying out the pathway for future triumphs.

Small Auspicious brings end goals that hold slightly longer time trajectories, but accompanied with the same staying power, success does ultimately come. Learn to celebrate the smallet of wins and stay clearheaded about your ultimate goals. If you constantly step back to examine the bigger picture, you will not lose sight of why you are doing what you're doing.

ENHANCER: Remember that *Stars of Big and Small Auspicious* bring the potential of great fortune, but to enjoy their benefits to the fullest, they need to be enhanced. Each year then, we design a Big Auspicious Enhancer to kickstart the very positive effects of these stars. This year, all animal signs benefit from displaying the **Six Birds Auspicious Multiplier**. This activator featuring an I-Ching coin with six birds and the auspicious amulet enhancer brings new opportunities. The 6 birds activates the #6 Heaven Star that rules the year's Lo Shu chart. The number 6 is the number of the heavens, which unlocks the celestial hand of the Gods. Display this potent activator in a place where you can see it often – either in a prominent place in the home, or in front of you on your work desk.

6 Birds Auspicious Multiplier. Unlocks the Big Auspicious luck of the year.

LUCK FROM THE HEAVENS

Two stars that further magnify the luck of the heavens are the **Golden Deity Star** and the **Star of the Heavenly Seal**. These land in the location of the **Horse** and the **Monkey**, bringing these two signs the luck of celestial fortunes. For these two signs, help comes without having to seek it. They enjoy the patronage of powerful mentors with many wishing to help them. They also have better instincts and can trust their own judgment more. For the Horse, as it also enjoys two Big Auspicious stars, little can go wrong as long as it stays judicious and diligent. The Monkey however needs to employ its trademark cunning to make the most of the Heaven Seal; it has to dodge the Yin House and Facing 3 Killings, but its main 24 Mountain star influence is extremely positive.

To make the most of these stars, we recommend that the Horse and Monkey invite in a **Golden Deity** into the home. Any Buddha, God or holy figure in line with your own faith will work. We particularly love **Kuan Yin, the Goddess of Mercy**, revered by Chinese all around the world. She is the female personification of the compassionate Buddha and brings wealth, health and happiness and protection from harm.

Kuan Yin

THE GENERAL STAR

The **Rooster** enjoys the General Star, which brings it power and authority, but unfortunately also fuels its short fuse and hot temper. But the Rooster this year has the very lucky #8 star, which enhances its fortunes and intrinsic energy. The Rooster as a sign does not suffer fool's gladly, so all these indications point to a Rooster that reigns supreme in 2021, but one who may be insufferable to those it considers "beneath" them, whether in intelligence or in status. To make the most of this star, all Roosters this year benefit from displaying the **Power Ru Yi**, the scepter of authority which boosts its command as boss or leader, while ensuring no disgruntled subordinates try to make trouble, or rivals rise up to try to displace it.

Star of the Yin House

This star brings danger of sickness and disease, and a general lack of energy to those it afflicts. It is particularly dangerous if one is already ill or elderly, or with other heavy afflictions indicated in their charts. This year, there are two Yin House stars and these arrive in the SW and North, affecting the **Sheep**, **Monkey** and **Rat**. All three of these signs are advised to take more care this year when it comes to health, well-being and safety. We strongly suggest that these signs carry protective amulets to shield them from the influence of malevolent spirits that may wreak havoc in their lives. Any of the **seed syllables Om, Ah or**

OM   AH   HUM

Hum will invoke the presence of the mighty Buddha, establishing a firm spiritual circumference of protection around the wearer.

If ill health is of particular concern, we recommend wearing and displaying **Health Amulets**. The **Wu Lou**, **Garuda Bird**, and the **Healing Deer**, bring precious cosmic protection. The deer is especially wonderful; this animal has always been associated with health, strength and vigor. It is also the animal that holds the solution to good health when all other methods have not seemed to work. There are many folk legends associated with the deer in all cultures, but in Chinese mythology, the deer is almost always shown accompanying Sau, the divine God of Longevity.

Healing Deer

The Robbery Star

This star brings money loss and betrayal and especially affects the **Tiger** in 2021. Those born under this sign need to be especially mindful not to get taken in by con men and getting cheated by others. There is higher chance of getting conned into undertaking bad investments. Business partners and associates could prove untrustworthy. It is also very important whenever one has this affliction to take care of personal safety. Robberies, muggings, petty thieves and street crime become more of a danger. This star also brings risk of becoming a victim of chance or collateral damage in somebody else's fight.

To counter this negative star, you need the image of the **Blue Rhino and Elephant** in the home, and you MUST carry the **Anti Robbery Amulet**. This protects against losing money and possessions. It is also important to protect against personal harm and injury; wear protective amulet at all times! Females in particular should avoid venturing out alone late at night or putting themselves under unnecessary risk; they should carry the **Nightspot Protection Amulet** for protection against petty crime.

Yearly Conflict & Yearly Killings

These stars bring obstacles to everything you do, making it difficult to make meaningful progress. These are the stars that can discourage you from remaining steadfast and keeping on your intended path. It throws up unexpected snags and hitches, and when left unchecked, can overwhelm one with feelings of depression and anxiety. These are negative stars that gather the slings and arrows of misfortune hurling them your way with some measure of ferocity. It is as such extremely important to take note of their location each year and take definite steps to neutralize them.

In 2021, the Yearly Killings star has landed in the **Dragon**'s location of SE1, and the Yearly Conflict Star visits the N3 sector, affecting the animal signs of **Rat** and **Ox**.

The *Yearly Killings Star* is deadlier and needs immediate action – we suggest that all Dragon-born and all those whose bedrooms or main door location are in the SE carry the **28 Hums Protection Wheel** and invite in the **Buddha image of Nangsi Zilnon Guru Rinpoche**. He is the warrior Buddha who completely overcomes all types of obstacles brought by the Yearly Killings.

28 Hums
Protection
Wheel

The *Yearly Conflict Star* makes everyone want to fight with you, bringing opposition to your ideas and making it difficult to see your projects through. Working in teams becomes especially difficult. At work, this could mean difficult colleagues and fierce politicking by workplace rivals. Those afflicted by this star could find themselves spending the better part of their time dodging potshots rather than focusing on their work. It makes work life very unpleasant, and the effects of this star can also permeate one's social and private life. This negative star arrives in the N3 sector affecting all whose main door or bedroom or office are located in this part of the home or office, and it affects Rat and Ox born people. Those affected by this affliction need to carry protection amulets and display the relevant cures. The **Dorje Drolo Scorpion Amulet** is especially helpful in this regard.

Natural Disaster Star

This star arrives in the East sector, affecting those who spend much time in this part of the home. This is the star that puts in you in harm's way – being at the wrong place at the wrong time. It brings all manner of natural misfortune including floods, fires, earthquakes, tsunamis, viruses and disease. If you are afflicted by this star, you MUST carry spiritual protection. ALL East-facing homes benefit from inviting in a statue of **Guru Rinpoche**, and all whose homes face East should wear the **Bhrum Pendant** which protects against all kinds of harm, illness, accidents and avoidable misfortune.

LUCK OF THE 12 ANIMAL SIGNS

Every animal sign is affected by a host of factors which change each year, producing a different basket of combinations which influence each individual sign's luck differently. Aside from the animal sign year you were born under, there are additional factors affecting your luck, but viewed together with these indications, anyone can alter the course of their lives and make intelligent decisions to maximize luck through any given year.

Here we summarize the broad outlook for the different animal signs, and in later chapters of this book, we go into greater depth and detail on what all of this means for you personally, depending on your heavenly stem, your home direction, your lunar mansion and your compatibilities.

The **HORSE** is blessed with extremely fortunate indications with the double *stars of Big Auspicious* and the *Star of Golden Deity* brought by the 24 Mountains Compass of 2021. This sign has great good fortune coming, which should more than make up for the unfortunate stars it had to endure in the last two years. The Horse is an energetic and restless sign full of passion and appetite for adventure, but the last couple of years will have made it difficult for it to pursue its desires. This year changes all of this; the Horse person will feel like a cloud has lifted, and as the year progresses, things get better and better. There are no unlucky indications at all, and the Victory Star #1 promises some very exciting new developments in the Horse's life.

The Horse should boost its fortunes with the **6 Birds Auspicious Multiplier** and benefits from displaying the **Desktop Flag of Victory** in its vicinity.

Desktop Flag of Victory

The **MONKEY** and **ROOSTER** are the signs enjoying the luckiest element luck indications. These two Metal signs have superlative Life Force and Spirit Essence, suggesting an inner determination that is unwavering. These signs know exactly what it is they want and how to go about getting it. Both Monkey and Rooster are known for their innate intelligence and ingenuity, and their already immense brainpower gets a big boost this year. The Monkey in particular enjoys very promising "success" luck; not only can it get what it wants, it receives plenty of recognition to go along with it too!

The **Rooster** can boost success luck by surrounding itself with the presence of the **Victorious Windhorse Carrying a Jewel**, as can the Monkey. Both these signs also have excellent indications from the 24 Mountains, with Monkey enjoying the *Heaven Seal* and Rooster benefitting from the *General Star*. The Monkey should carry the **Dragon Heavenly Seal Amulet** and the Rooster needs the **Ru Yi**.

Dragon
Heavenly Seal
Amulet

The sign that gets hit by the *Five Yellow* this year are the **DRAGON** and **SNAKE**. This indicates that these signs need to watch that the *wu wang* does not bring misfortune their way. The Five Yellow of 2021 sits in a Wood sector, which suggests it is NOT a deadly Five Yellow; nevertheless, the obstacles it brings can cause life to feel very unpleasant indeed and it should be strongly subdued.

Dragon and Snake this year need to carry the **Five Element Pagoda Amulet with Tree of Life** to combat the afflictive energy, turning obstacles into productive challenges, and transforming unfortunate outcomes into promising ones. Both Dragon and Snake are signs that thrive in adversity, gaining strength and shrewdness when the going gets tough. And the *wu wang* of this year can be metamorphosed into positive rather than negative results. The Snake should have the **6 Birds Auspicious Multiplier**, while the Dragon needs the **28 Hums Protection Wheel**.

The WOOD ELEMENT SIGNS of **TIGER** and **RABBIT** both enjoy very good element indications but need to boost success luck with the **Victorious Windhorse** this year. The Tiger benefits from the *Small Auspicious*, and direct access to the hidden wealth of the year, but the Rabbit needs to do more work to boost its prosperity potential. The Tiger should display the **6 Birds Auspicious Multiplier** while the Rabbit MUST carry the **Three Celestial Shields Amulet** to stay protected against the 3 Killings affliction that affects it this year.

The WATER ELEMENT SIGNS of **RAT** and **BOAR** are the most unfortunate in terms of element luck, facing very bad life force and spirit essence. This can cause a sudden lack of confidence in one's own abilities and make these two signs prone to being easily discouraged. What the Rat and Boar need this year are strong cures to lift their inner energies. They need to carry the **Life Force Amulet** and **"Om" Dakini Spirit Enhancing Amulet**. What these two signs do have however are a shared *Big Auspicious Star*. Rat and Boar working together can produce very favourable results, and their affinity with each other gets enhanced this year. These two signs will make good business partners. Of the two, Rat will be luckier than Boar, and should take the lead in any endeavor they embark on together.

The EARTH SIGNS of **OX**, **DOG**, **DRAGON** and **SHEEP** all have good life force but bad spirit essence. This suggests that for these signs, they have decent inherent energy, but exposure to the wrong company could be harmful to their mindsets and their motivation levels. They are spiritually weaker than usual and need to carry the **"Om" Dakini Spirit Enhancing Amulet**. Those who are spiritual in nature can draw strength from their belief systems and find solace and comfort in their spiritual practice.

The **SHEEP** meanwhile is also in direct clash with the TAI SUI of the year, and hence the priority for this sign should be to take all steps to appease the God of the Year. The Sheep needs the **Tai Sui Amulet**, and its celestial guardian animal this year should be the **Dragon Pi Yao**. The

Tai Sui Amulet

Sheep can lean on its special friend the Horse, who enjoys superlative luck in 2021. The Sheep working or hanging out with a Horse in the coming year will benefit tremendously from its astrological soulmate. But all four Earth signs are in direct or indirect conflict with the Year God and should thus ALL carry the **Tai Sui Amulet** and have his plaque in the home.

WEALTH LUCK IN 2021

Wealth luck this coming year is weak. It will be difficult to make quick money. Wealth that gets created will come from hard work rather than speculative gains. The year continues to see much disruption to the way business is done, making things difficult for those in sunset industries. Individuals who can spot new opportunities can profit, but increasingly, the free flow of information will reduce the time window for monopolies in new industries. It will be creativity and originality, together with consistent hard work that will allow individuals and businesses to generate income in 2021.

As machines take over more and more jobs, those who do not do something and stubbornly hang on to an old way of life could quickly find themselves being made redundant. The year will not be an easy one for wealth creation, and macro level events continue to depress the immediate outlook.

Certain animal signs will have element luck in their

favour when it comes to wealth luck this year; even so, the advice is to weigh all decisions carefully before making them. This is a year when one can take risks, but do not put all your eggs in one basket. Make sure any risks taken are calculated ones backed by understanding and research.

WEALTH ENHANCER: All individuals benefit from inviting in wealth enhancers, particularly the **Asset Wealth Bull** which boosts money and income luck, but also protects against your assets losing value. Those invested in the stock market would benefit greatly from the presence of this bull in the home. It has been designed to look like the stock market bull on Wall Street and carries the meaning "May the market bull for you"; it also features auspicious symbols of good fortune, a red saddle to represent prosperity in 2021, and it is shown presiding over a pile of coins and ingots, signifying its control and dominance over cash. With this bull, you will always have enough money, and even those who sustain losses will quickly make it back.

Asset Wealth Bull

GETTING YOUR TIMING RIGHT:
The Dragon sign in 2021 benefits very much from keeping the **"Green Dragon" Constellation Lucky Charms** nearby. This awakens all the positive attributes of the Dragon – charisma, courage, ambition, leadership and most important for the Dragon sign this year, great energy. The Dragon enjoys excellent success luck, but your weak life force and inner essence will make you tend to give up easily when things do not go according to plan. Activating the Dragon's Lunar Constellation ensures you get your timing right when making important decisions, and when acting on them. It will also boost your grit and staying power in a year when your opportunities are there, but one where you may take some effort spotting them.

"Green Dragon" Constellation Lucky Charms

LOVE LUCK IN 2021
SINGLES CAN FIND LOVE IN 2021

For singles, this is a promising year for romance. The *Peach Blossom Star* has settled into the East, a WOOD sector, which gives it strength. The East is also the palace of the Rabbit, which is associated with the

Moon and Moon Goddess who presides over fortunes related to love and romance. She bestows wishes to do with relationships, aids in matchmaking soulmates, and improves relations between married couples.

In 2021, the East becomes the place of the "Moon Rabbit" and enhancing this sector manifests love and romance for those looking for true love in their lives. Those wishing to settle down and get married, or searching for their soulmate or one true love, displaying the **Rabbit in the Moon** in the East will manifest this kind of luck for you.

MARRIED COUPLES BEWARE!!!

While there will be plenty of love and romance in 2021, it will not always be the kind that brings happiness. The year's chart also features the *Flower of Romance Star*. Unfortunately, it is the "external" version of this star – making all marriages vulnerable as there will be too much temptation from outside. Innocent flirtations can get out of hand, after-work drinks with colleagues or out-of-town business conferences can lead to inappropriate entanglements, spouses with the seven-year itch could be tempted to act on it. This is a year when those who are married should pay more attention to their other halves.

The *External Star of Romance* often affect those who have grown to take their marriage for granted. As long as you realise it, you can start taking measures to make things right. But what if an affair has already started?

CURE: We advise that when this troublesome star is present, married couples should make an effort to display symbols of marital stability and happiness in the home. All married couples should have the **Marriage Happiness Ducks** in the home, in the SW, East or center. Each can also carry the **Enhancing Relationships Amulet** to protect against third parties elbowing their way in and "crowding" the marriage.

Displaying the **"Rabbit in the Moon" Love Enhancer** in the home is also an excellent protective measure against stars that affect marital peace and happiness. In 2021, all couples can safeguard their marriage by displaying the Moon Rabbit with the full moon in the East part of their home. For those who suspect their spouse is already cheating, you can call on the help of **Kurukulle**, the powerful Goddess of Love. Invoking her presence in your life imbues you with her talent for enchantment, giving you your power back when it comes to your spouse and your marriage. You can display her **Banner of Love** or carry the **Red Tara Home Protection Amulet** – this powerful talisman designed with her image and all her implements of love will repair damage already done to your marriage, while strengthening the bond between you and your spouse. Kurukulle's powers of magnetism will also make it difficult for others to adversely affect your marriage.

We also advise chanting her mantra daily:
OM KURUKULLE HRIH SOHA (21 times or 108 times)

STUDY LUCK IN 2021

To enhance study luck in 2021, students should call on the help of **Manjushri**, the Buddha of Wisdom. Manjushri with his wisdom sword slices through all ignorance in the mind, enhancing one's wisdom and knowledge. Invoking his help benefits not just students and those studying for exams, but also anyone needing to make important decisions and life choices. He clears the mind to make way for effective and efficient accumulation of knowledge – so that "your knowledge is vast, and your understanding complete". This year we have designed a **Manjushri Home Amulet** for scholars and students to place on their study desk. Manjushri's seed syllable is "DHIH" and chanting this repeatedly in one breath until you run out of breath is the best way to invoke his presence.

You can also chant Manjushri's wisdom mantra:
OM AH RAPA CHA NA DHIH

Make it a habit to chant his mantra either 21 times or 108 times (1 mala) before you sleep each night, or when you can find some quiet time during the day. We suggest you get yourself a **Manjushri Wisdom Mala** which you reserve specially for this purpose – chanting only Manjushri's Wisdom Mantra. This sharpens the mala's power and effectiveness when it comes to study luck, as the energies you direct into the mala as you chant becomes concentrated, making it more and more potent the more you use it.

HEALTH LUCK IN 2021

The Illness Star has flown into the North, the sector of the Rat. This affects all those born in Rat years, but also those whose main doors or bedrooms are located in the North of the home, or those who spend a lot of time in the North sector. Those afflicted with sickness or health problems should have the **Healing Deer** in the North.

Health risks continue to look like a threat going into 2021 so we have designed several potent health and protective talismans to keep everyone safe.

Our **mantra ring** this year features Medicine Buddha's mantra on the outside and Vairocana's mantra on the inside. Medicine Buddha comes to the aid of anyone who is sick and who calls to him for help. Vairocana is the Buddha that protects against contagious diseases. COVID-19 has been a life-altering phenomenon for the whole world throughout the last year, and as we move into 2021, it does not look like things will revert quite back to normal. We need to continue to practise vigilance following new guidelines as they get discovered to keep safe. Mask up, keep your social distance and get used to a new way of living.

The science of feng shui meanwhile always advocates protection before enhancement, so we strongly advise everyone irrespective of their animal signs to always wear or carry health and protective amulets. It can literally save your life!

The **Medicine Buddha-Vairocana Mantra Ring** is excellent to help keep you safe during these strange and troubled times.

This year we also strongly recommend the **Health Talisman with Tortoise and Snake**. The Tortoise and Snake are two spiritual creatures associated with longevity, known for their potent powers to heal. The tortoise provides stability both in physical and mental health, while the Snake represents control over the nagas, spirits that can cause ill health and sickness when they are left to their own mischievous devices.

All signs whose element luck tables indicate a poor health category should also place these health cures near to them or carry as portable amulets.

Element Luck of the Dragon in 2021
Chapter 2

- Water Dragon – 9 & 69 years
- Metal Dragon – 21 & 81 years
- Earth Dragon – 33 & 93 years
- Fire Dragon – 45 years
- Wood Dragon – 57 years

ELEMENT LUCK OF THE DRAGON IN 2021

The Dragon's element luck chart indicates incredible success potential in 2021, but while your propensity for success is high, you have to deal with a poor level of spirit essence. What this suggests is that while you may have big dreams and potential, you may lack the staying power this year. You need to work on finishing what you start, and on not getting discouraged before you are finished.

The other indications in your chart suggest that there will be many obstacles along the way. The *Five Yellow* certainly needs addressing, and you also have some worrisome 24 mountains indications to deal with. But your element luck will help you in 2021, so you need to do everything you can to make the most of this luck.

The key phrase for the Dragon this year is DO NOT GIVE UP!

While the Dragon is a dynamic sign, always the first to come up with grand new ideas and to act on them, Dragons are also easily distracted. When the going gets tough, Dragons find it tempting to abandon what they are finding difficult, and simply move on to the next thing. In 2021, the Dragon needs to stay focused

ELEMENT LUCK OF

	METAL DRAGON 81/21 years	WATER DRAGON 69/9 years	WOOD DRAGON 57 years
Life Force	good ☼	good ☼	good ☼
Health	excellent ☼☼☼	very bad xx	neutral ☼x
Wealth	bad x	excellent ☼☼☼	very bad xx
Success	excellent ☼☼☼	excellent ☼☼☼	excellent ☼☼☼
Spirit Essence	bad x	bad x	bad x

THE DRAGON IN 2021

FIRE DRAGON 45 years	EARTH DRAGON 33 years	2021 Element
good ☺	good ☺	Earth
good ☺	very good ☺☺	Earth
very good ☺☺	neutral ☺✗	Metal
excellent ☺☺☺	excellent ☺☺☺	Water
bad ✗	bad ✗	Fire

and committed to tasks once they begin them. This does not mean you cannot have more than one thing on your plate – a Dragon is the master juggler, able to handle a myriad different responsibilities at once, but you must not abandon what you start. Or you will find you never finish anything.

There is no harm taking a break from something when you hit a mental block, but come back to it. Do not allow yourself to be influenced by wet blankets or do-gooders offering you bad advice. Listen to your instincts. Your ideas may be wild, but only to those who do not have your vision and who cannot see what you can. Keep trusting yourself and give more weight to your own judgement. For the Dragon in 2021, there is nothing more important than having unwavering confidence and belief in yourself.

The Dragon this year can lean on its astrological ally the Monkey. Every animal sign belongs to a Trinity in the Chinese Zodiac, and in years when one's luck is compromised, one can draw strength on the good fortune of an allied animal sign. The Dragon belongs to the Trinity of Competitors comprising also the Rat and Monkey; in 2021, the strongest of these three signs is the Monkey, who has truly excellent element indications. One way the Dragon can benefit from the Monkey's good energies is by displaying **images of the Monkey** in your living space.

This year it benefits all Dragon-born to display images of your astrological ally the MONKEY in the home.

Collaborating with those born in Monkey years also brings good fortune to the Dragon in 2021. If you are working with a Monkey, have a child who is a Monkey-born, or have friends born under this sign, there is a good chance they will be a very good influence over you this year.

Surround yourself with friends who build you up. Avoid those who constantly dent your confidence. The last thing you need is to feel fragile or weak. For the Dragon, you have great capacity to achieve great things in 2021, and it will happen for those of you who do not let anything knock your self-assurance.

Activate your EXCELLENT success potential with the **Victorious Windhorse Carrying a Jewel**. The magical Windhorse is the physical representation and embodiment of one's success potential, and this year when this category of your luck is so exceptional, you should do everything to activate this. Have images of the Windhorse around you and also carry with you at all times as an amulet hanging or gold card in your wallet.

Because your spirit essence is weak this year, you must work at improving this. You can use element therapy by boosting Earth energy around you. You can do this by wearing Earth colours which include all the earth tones and all shades of yellow. You can also use natural crystals. Wear yellow gemstones and have crystals in your living space.

Earth element energy always enhances the Dragon sign, as your intrinsic element is Earth, but in 2021 it also improves your spirit essence, the inner essence that gives you your self-confidence and conviction.

You should also carry the **"Om" Dakini Spirit Enhancing Amulet**. This works at boosting this category of your element luck, the main category that is under par this year.

WEALTH LUCK FOR THE DIFFERENT DRAGONS

Wealth luck differs for the different element Dragons, but especially benefits the **69-year-old Metal Dragon** and the **45-year-old Fire Dragon** in 2021. These two Dragons enjoy excellent element wealth luck, which suggests that financially, you will be very comfortable this year and your wealth can grow. To take fullest advantage, you should display the **Tree Bringing 3 Kinds of Wealth** in your living space; this will add growth energy to your wealth potential, boosting career and investment luck, and for some of you even attract a windfall.

The **33-year-old Earth Dragon** has good element wealth luck, suggesting your finances will be stable. There is money to be made even if it may not be BIG money. Don't be hasty to make big money. Your time will come. For now, work at steadily achieving success.

The **21-year-old and 81-year-old Metal Dragons** have a less robust indication in the wealth luck category. The advice for these Dragons is to steer clear of risky investments. For these Dragons, the best strategy is to ensure you maintain a sufficiently diversified portfolio and do not succumb to taking financial risks, no matter how irresistible, as luck is not on your side with wealth prospects.

The **57-year-old Wood Dragon** has its wealth category at a VERY BAD level, so this is a warning to take serious steps to preserve your wealth. Avoid risky plays when it comes to money matters. This is not a year for frivolous expenditures. Unexpected and unavoidable expenses could crop up, disrupting your personal financial plan for the year. Make adjustments as needed and stay frugal. This Dragon needs the **"Hum" Dakini Wealth Protection Amulet** to safeguard your wealth.

HEALTH OF THE DRAGON

The only Dragon with anything serious to worry about when it comes to health this year is the **69-year-old**

Water Dragon. For this Dragon, you should pay more attention to your health. Go for your regular check-ups. If you don't feel well for any reason, get it looked at. Do not leave health concerns to a point when it is too late to do anything about it. For the 69-year-old Dragon, because you are also not young anymore, you must not take your health for granted.

This Dragon should carry the **Health Talisman Holder with Health Mantras** at all times and have the **Medicine Buddha and the 7 Sugatas Gau** near you. Do not expose yourself to infectious viruses and diseases; with the COVID19 threat for example, you must absolutely not take any risks when it comes to your health. If there are quarantine recommendations in place, follow them. Don't be foolhardy and think you are invincible because this year, health-wise, you are not.

The Dragon enjoys EXCELLENT levels of SUCCESS LUCK in 2021, indicating your achievements can be big, impactful and lasting. But you need to overcome your weak spirit essence to ensure your success potential is not derailed by a lack of self-confidence and staying power.

WATER DRAGON 9 year old	
life force	good ☉
health	very bad xx
wealth	excellent ☉☉☉
success	excellent ☉☉☉
spirit essence	bad x

THE 9-YEAR-OLD WATER DRAGON

The Dragon child is a most precious child, because he or she is believed to bring good luck to any family he belongs to. The happy and positive demeanour of any Dragon-born rubs off on everyone he or she comes into contact with, and this is even more so when it comes to Dragon children. They are a breath of fresh air! The coming year looks like an excellent one for Dragon children in terms of success and attainments, so this year sees them develop confidence in new skills and abilities.

The only concern is the poor showing in the health category of this Dragon. It is important for parents of young Dragon children to take their health concerns seriously this year. Do not ignore warning signs and it is better to be safe than sorry. Encourage your Dragon child to lead a healthy lifestyle – get exercise each day, eat a balanced diet, get enough sleep, have a good balance between schoolwork and play.

The 9-year-old Dragon benefits from **Manjushri**, the Buddha of Wisdom. Manjushri is the patron saint of education and blesses all trying to better themselves and to acquire knowledge and understanding. This Dragon should also wear a **Health Amulet** to counter the weak element luck in this category, or clip one onto their schoolbag.

METAL DRAGON 21 year old	
life force	good o
health	excellent ooo
wealth	bad x
success	excellent ooo
spirit essence	bad x

THE 21-YEAR-OLD METAL DRAGON

For the **21-year-old Metal Dragon**, this is a year when it is easy for you to achieve success at college and in your studies. You are feeling vibrant and alive, with excellent physical health and vitality. Creativity is at a high, allowing you to make breakthroughs in research and knowledge accumulation. Those who throw themselves into their studies can attain impressive scholastic accolades that will set them up well for the next stage in life.

This is not however the time for this Dragon to

get sidetracked by entrepreneurial activities, as wealth luck in 2021 is lacking. Those trying to make money on the side may find themselves less successful here, so it is best to stay focused on scholastic endeavours. Earning a side income to support one's studies or daily needs may be commendable, but this year, it is prudent for this Dragon to err on the side of caution when it comes to commercial ventures. Do not risk your own money because it is easy to lose it! And don't dilute your focus compromising your performance in your studies.

The young Dragon is impetuous, headstrong and sometimes hasty in its decision-making. Be sure to think things through before rushing into anything, and do not allow your judgement to be clouded by the opinions of too many.

This Dragon is always surrounded by friends, and is usually the ringleader, dominating its pals rather than the other way around. But because this is a year when your spirit essence is weak, it leaves you vulnerable to being dissuaded from what you truly believe in. This can result in you beginning to feel uncertain about your own choices, and indecisiveness could creep in.

Take a step back whenever someone else causes you to change your mind. Mull things over and make up your own mind rather than reacting permaturely and unwisely to the opinions of others.

Success luck is excellent for this young Dragon, so it is worthwhile to stay focused on a set number of definitive goals. It is often tempting for the Dragon to have too many things on the go at once, because you are so naturally talented at so many things! But to achieve excellence, it is important to direct your efforts to what is important. Don't fall into the trap of becoming a jack of all trades and a master of none. You have superlative success luck this year; do not waste it.

This Dragon benefits from the **Dragon Tortoise**, who will keep you grounded in a time when there are too many things on offer. The Dragon Tortoise is an excellent symbol for young people in college or just entering the working world – it attracts the support you need from those who can help you, and lends you the wisdom and maturity that will help you at this stage in your life.

EARTH DRAGON 33 year old	
life force	good ○
health	very good ○○
wealth	**neutral** **ox**
success	excellent ○○○
spirit essence	bad x

THE 33-YEAR-OLD EARTH DRAGON

This Earth Dragon is going through an excellent year when your element luck is firmly on your side. All categories of luck are exceedingly promising, suggesting you can make a success of anything you try your hand at. Wealth luck is good, so there is money to be made. Health luck is very good, which ensures you will not lose steam along the way due to physical weakness. Best of all, your *lung ta* is at an excellent level, indicating you can achieve the very highest levels of success.

This is a year when this Dragon can start something new, make a difference, leave your mark. Without financial worries, you can indulge in passion projects as you will not have to worry about putting food on the table. If there is something you have always wanted to get started on, you find yourself with the time and conviction to follow up. You also have no problem harnessing the support you need.

What you do have to do is to strengthen your spirit essence, which has a weak showing. You can do this by carrying the **"Om" Dakini Spirit Enhancing Amulet**. Do not allow yourself to be discouraged by obstacles that may crop up along the way; the size of these hindrances will depend on how you view them. Mental strength, of which you have plenty, will ensure you look on setbacks as opportunities to learn from, rather than anything that can stand in your way.

2021 looks very promising for this category of Dragon. Your Earth element heavenly stem ensures you stay grounded, so even while you are dreaming up big ideas that can change the world, you find solutions that are practical and pragmatic, the kind that garners you easy support from those you need help from.

This Dragon benefits from the **Bejewelled Dragon Ru Yi**. This Ru Yi gives you the mental strength and authority to get others onto your side, helping you win allies and supporters who will prove invaluable to you this year. It also brings you the power of the Double Dragon, activating your intrinsic energies and strengthening your mental powers and inner strength.

To ensure you always get your timing right, carry the **"Green Dragon" Lunar Mansions Talisman**. Excellent for those in business, who play the stock market, or who are involved in any monetary risks.

FIRE DRAGON 45 year old	
life force	good ○
health	good ○
wealth	very good ○○
success	excellent ○○○
spirit essence	bad x

THE 45-YEAR-OLD FIRE DRAGON

Of all your Dragon siblings, you are the most headstrong and competitive. You are always dreaming up big ideas and as you set the bar very high for yourself, you expect the same from everyone around you. This may not always make you the most popular person, but you can get things done. You have enormous energy, and this year, this inner vitality of yours gets enhanced. Your Fire element heavenly stem adds fuel to everything you put your mind to, and this year, it attracts wealth luck into your orbit.

This is an excellent year for this Dragon to turn its attention to commercial endeavours and anything to do with making money. Prosperity luck is promising, and you can be as brave and as financially aggressive as you want when it comes to financial matters. You can look at new investment opportunities seriously, and also consider offers of new employment that come your way.

Opportunities to relocate or change jobs can bring exciting new growth opportunities. This is a year when you will not be short of new wealth enhancement proposals being brought to you for consideration. Good things make their way to your doorstep, so it is an excellent year to stay alert to opportunities.

You are on a roll career-wise.

This is a year to give serious thought to reshaping your future should the chance to do so appear. The outlook is exceedingly positive, so do direct attention on your personal ambitions and consider everything that is put on the table. There is great benefit to putting your heart towards making quantum leaps in your professional growth this year.

As well as very positive indications when it comes to wealth, you also enjoy excellent success luck. Your lung ta is at its very highest level, which suggests that the outlook of what you can achieve is incredibly exciting. You are feeling very motivated, so what you need to do now is start to act on those motivations. The only drawback for this Dragon is your fast temper; watch that in your zeal and enthusiasm, you do not tread on other people's egos if they do not agree with you, or if they cannot keep up with your pace. The last thing this Dragon needs is to make unnecessary enemies.

This Dragon should have the **Windhorse Success Talisman** to ensure your excellent success luck gets fully activated. You should also have the **Five Element Pagoda with Tree of Life** nearby at all times – best to carry the amulet version to stay constantly protected against the *wu wang*, which is the one affliction the Dragon has to be very aware of this year.

WOOD DRAGON 57 year old	
life force	good ⚬
health	**neutral** ox
wealth	very bad xx
success	excellent ⚬⚬⚬
spirit essence	bad x

THE 57-YEAR-OLD WOOD DRAGON

The Wood Dragon does not have such a stellar prediction from its element luck tables. Like your Dragon siblings, you enjoy excellent success luck, but your wealth luck is very bad and your health luck neutral.

This is a year when you need to beware of taking too many financial risks. This Dragon is a natural risk-taker, but your appetite for high-risk-high-return opportunities may get you into trouble. Refrain from speculating on the stock market, and do not gamble this year! You can win, but you can also lose big!

This Dragon needs to protect its wealth this year, so we recommend **Wealth Cabinets** to ensure you can accumulate what you make. These symbolise your wealth growing rather than depleting over the course of the year.

The Wood Dragon in 2021 should not just go with the flow. Make active decisions rather than allowing things to settle into their own equilibrium. Because your luck is not perfect, you need to work at actively changing that luck. Give your input into decision-making processes that involve you, engage that formidable brain of yours, don't get lazy!

The Wood Dragon is an inspired and exploratory creature, and this is a year when these natural aptitudes of your sign will prove invaluable - but you must engage them.

Your health luck is only neutral, so do make an effort to lead a healthy lifestyle. Get enough rest and don't overexert yourself physically. Those not careful to pace themselves could pick up an avoidable injury that could make life cumbersome over the course of the year. An excellent symbol for this Dragon is the **Double Fish**. This symbol will help you avert accidents, epidemics and poor health. It will also attract abundance into your life at a time when your wealth luck is lacking. You can also wear the **Medicine Buddha - Vairocana Mantra Ring** to protect against all forms of health threats.

This Dragon should limit any risk-taking or speculative activity on the stock market as your wealth indication is very poorly. Carry the **"Hum" Dakini Wealth Protection Amulet**.

WATER DRAGON 69 year old	
life force	good o
health	very bad xx
wealth	excellent ooo
success	excellent ooo
spirit essence	bad x

THE 69-YEAR-OLD WATER DRAGON

This wise old Dragon enjoys a year with excellent wealth and success luck, but health luck is less robust. You have no financial worries, so do not overexert yourself when it comes to work matters. Do not allow yourself to get stressed out for any reason. Learn to take things easy and to enjoy your family and friends. Because your health is not so robust, it is prudent to be more careful when it comes to epidemics and pandemics. Viruses like COVID19 become more dangerous for you, so for this Dragon, you need to be more thorough when it comes to protecting yourself.

This Dragon should wear **Health Amulets** at all times as a safeguard against your poor health showing. An excellent amulet is the **Prayer Wheel Pendant for Health**. This prayer wheel is filled with the mantra of Medicine Buddha who protects against sickness and disease. You should also engage the **Buddha Vairocana**, who protects against pandemics. Invite Vairocana into your home and even better if you learn up his mantra and chant regularly – his full mantra is available on *www.chantamantra.com*

Wealth luck looks excellent in 2021, so there are good gains to be made from your investments. Whatever you give your support to this year will thrive and do very well. Money matters are looking good so there is little to worry about here. But because health luck is weak, it is best not to let the small things worry you - so it may be better to avoid those exciting gambles you may have taken in your youth. Best not to engage in anything that may make your heart pound too quickly!

A wonderful year however to devote to a cause you believe you. Your ability to galvanize others and to bring people together has not faded and working towards a cause will bring new meaning into your life. It will also make you a host of new friends and bring a welcome change of energy.

METAL DRAGON 81 year old	
life force	good o
health	excellent ooo
wealth	bad x
success	excellent ooo
spirit essence	bad x

THE 81-YEAR-OLD METAL DRAGON

The **81-year-old Metal Dragon** has a smooth year ahead. Your health element luck is excellent, so there shouldn't be anything major to worry about here. This is a good indication for someone your age, as it means you have the physical condition that makes for a very pleasant year. Indeed, there is nothing more welcome in one's latter years than good and strong physical

health. Living becomes easier and all the aches and pains that come with old age become much more bearable then.

This is a year when you can enjoy yourself indulging in activities that engage the mind. You are feeling alert and mentally agile, so the more you have to sink your teeth into, the better you will feel. Your wealth element luck is weak, so do not take risks financially. But otherwise, your fortunes this year look extremely promising, indicating a time for enjoyment and personal growth, in more spiritual dimensions perhaps.

The Metal Dragon is the most physically active of all the Dragons, so even at your age, you won't be content to sit still. Continue incorporating fitness and exercise into your daily routine, even if mild. You are also a sociable creature, so do not retreat into your own company, as you don't take well to that. Even in a world when social distancing has become a common term, regularly meet with friends and family, even if only through video calls and the internet.

This Dragon should wear the **Medicine Buddha - Vairocana Mantra Ring** for longevity and health. You also benefit from **Vajrasattva's Mantra Wand**. Vajrasattva purifies all negativities in your life, removing obstacles to happiness and good luck.

Four Pillars Chart 2021

Chapter 3

FOUR PILLARS CHART 2021

An important indicator of the potential of any year is the Four Pillars chart of the year. This reveals the impact of the five elements of the year. When all five elements are present, it indicates a balance, a preferred situation. In feng shui, we are always striving for balance, and when something is out of balance, we always endeavor to bring things back into balance by introducing the missing element. This year, the chart

HOUR	DAY	MONTH	YEAR
壬	癸	庚	辛
Yang Water	Yin Water	Yang Metal	Yin Metal
壬 子	己 未	甲 寅	己 丑
Yang Water Rat	Yin Earth Sheep	Yang Wood Tiger	Yin Earth Ox

This year's Four Pillars chart lacks Fire, the element that signifies wealth luck.

is obviously missing Fire, the element that indicates WEALTH LUCK, so the year lacks opportunities to make money.

However, the eight characters in the Four Pillars – made up of 4 heavenly stems and 4 earthly branches – are not the only elements present. The interaction of these elements, depending on where and how they are positioned within the chart, generates a set of hidden elements as well as special stars. We use this chapter to analyse each part of this year's Four Pillars chart, and mention the most significant findings.

2021's Paht Chee chart indicates a strong self-element of Water, which boosts competitive energies and puts everyone on edge. Friends become foes when the stakes are raised, so this is a year to constantly watch one's back. The year's chart is unbalanced; it is missing the vital element of FIRE, which represents wealth and financial success. It is thus a year when it will be difficult to make much headway in the creation of new wealth. Profits may take a long time to get realized and there are few speculative gains to be made.

Prosperity comes with hard work rather than with a stroke of luck. This is definitely not a year to strike it rich via the lottery.

Here is a closer look at the most important indications this year:

HOUR	DAY	MONTH	YEAR
壬 Yang Water	癸 Yin Water	庚 Yang Metal	辛 Yin Metal
壬子 Yang Water Rat	己未 Yin Earth Sheep	甲寅 Yang Wood Tiger	己丑 Yin Earth Ox

There appears to be way too much Water in this year's chart.

A YEAR OF STRONG WATER
indicating a competitive year

First, the self-element of the year is Strong Water. It is a year when rivalry becomes enhanced and when politics can get unscrupulous. Watch your back and reserve your trust for your very innermost circle. Indeed, even your inner circle could let you down if the circumstances dictate. Betrayals happen of their own accord, sometimes without the guilty party's conscious intention. Learn to forgive and move on but protect yourself by being more careful and by putting safeguards in place. Remove temptation where you can and stay close to all you are working with.

PROTECTION: Those in business are advised to carry the **Kuan Kung on Horseback Anti-Betrayal Amulet**. This will protect you against the betrayal of others and being let down by people whom you trust. It keeps you prepared for whatever the winds and waters bring your way.

In any competitive endeavour, it could well feel like a fight to the death. Diplomatic compromises will be difficult to achieve, and different factions and interest groups find it harder to reach win-win scenarios. But it is nevertheless important to try. Sometimes being the bigger person will help; but recognize when you have to fight and when you don't. Indeed, do not mistakenly think you are in fact being the magnanimous one when you are being taken for a fool. It is a year when it is prudent to carry protection always. The **28 Hums Protection Amulet** is an excellent all-round amulet that will safeguard you from all kinds of harm.

SOLUTION: The excess of Water energy in the chart needs to be resolved. Use **WOOD energy** to weaken the excess Water. Having plenty of greenery and live plants in your living space will help re-balance the energies and will also bring vital growth energy to a year which lacks the presence of the *Lap Chun*, or "Spring".

This year, having plenty of plants and Wood energy in the home around you will help soak up the excess Water in the year's chart.

BALANCE OF YIN & YANG

Second, there are two Yang pillars and two Yin Pillars.
There is thus a good mix between energetic periods
and restive ones, with no dominance of work over
play, or vice versa. The Yang Month and Hour Pillars
bring great vitality, while the Yin Year and Day Pillars
bring balance. There should be more than enough
strength to propel positive chi forward and upward.
People in general are open to different viewpoints.
If negative energies can be kept under control and
sufficiently subdued, the year is then able to propel
forward, benefitting many.

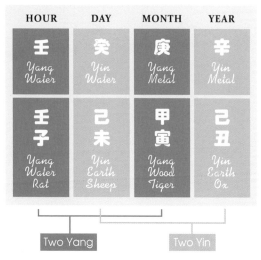

This year there is good balance between Yang and Yin
in the year's Four Pillars chart.

CLASH OF SHEEP WITH OX
indicating strong conflict energy

Third, there is a clash of SHEEP with OX in the Earth Branches. This clash between two Earth animals suggests that the clash will be between leaders. Earth is the element that represents leadership and rank, thus animosity will likely be between those who are in charge. But because those in power are especially strong this year, fighting can become ferocious, with the damage dealt far-reaching. There will be strong clashes between the leaders of nations.

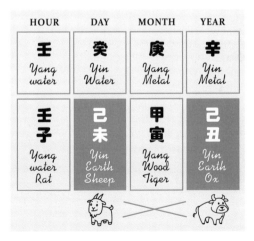

The clash between Ox and Sheep brings many problems to the year, especially between those who are in charge and everyone else who could end up as collateral damage.

Within family units, because the clash occurs in the Day Pillar, there is likely to be strong conflict between spouses.

SOLUTION: There may be more marital problems in 2021 with the Sheep in the Self-Spouse pillar clashing with the Year pillar. In the family unit, this coupled with the presence of the *External Flower of Romance* star brings all kinds of problems to husband and wife. Every home this year should have the **"Rabbit in the Moon" Love Enhancer** and better still if both husband and wife carry the **Enhancing Relationships Amulet**. Recognize when an outsider is trying to make trouble in your marriage, and refrain from siding with a third party over your spouse, no matter how much your husband or wife may be annoying you. When you allow an outsider into the mix, this year, such troubles can escalate very quickly.

Enhancing Relationships Amulet

SPECIAL LINK BETWEEN RAT & OX
bringing creativity and inventiveness

Fourth, there is however a very strong affinity between RAT and OX in the Earthly Branches of the Year and Hour Pillar. This is a heaven sent because it serves to repair some of the damage resulting from the Ox-Sheep clash. The Year Pillar of the Ox forms a soulmate pairing with the Hour Pillar of the Rat, which means there is a good beginning and a good ending to the year, what the Chinese refer to as having a head and tail, a suggestion that things that

HOUR	DAY	MONTH	YEAR
壬	癸	庚	辛
Yang Water	Yin Water	Yang Metal	Yin Metal
壬 子	己 未	甲 寅	己 丑
Yang Water Rat	Yin Earth Sheep	Yang Wood Tiger	Yin Earth Ox

The Rat and Ox in this year's chart forms a very special affinity, bringing relationship and completion luck.

get started have a good chance to reach satisfactory completion. The two signs of Rat and Ox are extremely harmonious together, generating the *House of Cleverness and Creativity*, with the Rat starting and the Ox completing. This endows the year with wonderful ingenuity and inventiveness.

> *The presence of the Rat & Ox in the year's Four Pillars suggests a year when true friendship means something.*

These two signs are also a secret-friend pair, indicating **good friendship luck** through the year. While there are indications of strong competition and rivalry, there is also much potential for firm friendships, and opportunities for friends to demonstrate their loyalties and allegiance. A year perhaps of finding out who one's true friends are.

ENHANCER: Get the **"Perfect Partnerships to Attract Big Wealth" Enhancer**. This enhancer featuring the Ox and Rat will boost all the positive indications of this combination. Display in a prominent area in the home; in the living room, or near the dining room where you spend a lot of time. The number "8" on the Ox activates for the missing wealth luck of the year.

NO PROSPERITY LUCK INDICATED
... but there is hidden wealth

Fifth, there is MISSING WEALTH. Fire which represents wealth is completely missing from the main chart. What this indicates is that it will be difficult to make money. New businesses will take time getting off the ground, sales will be slow, industries that are shrinking will continue to do so, while their replacements will take time to take flight. Profit margins get squeezed as information becomes more and more freely available, and technology continues to disrupt at breakneck pace. This year, if one wants to stay afloat, it is vitally important to keep up with the world that is so rapidly changing around us.

While there will be results and completions, it will nevertheless feel like an interim year, because we are at the beginning end of a new cycle, and not quite at the close of the current period. 2021 represents the second animal sign of the cycle after the new decade last year opened with the Rat, and we are heading towards the end of Period 8, and the beginning of Period 9, but we are not quite there yet.

There is a lack of obvious wealth in 2021, but those who look hard can find gold. This year, there is HIDDEN WEALTH brought by the sign of the TIGER.

While WEALTH luck may be lacking, there is however HIDDEN WEALTH brought by the TIGER. This will bring some respite, and keep us tided over, but it is wealth that comes in its own time rather than overnight. What this means is that 2021 is a year when we can lay the foundations for future wealth, but we must not get our hopes up for immediate results.

That the hidden wealth star is brought by the Tiger bodes well for friends of the Tiger – the Dog and especially the Horse.

The Dog enjoys one *Small Auspicious Star* from the 24 mountains chart, while the Horse enjoys not one but *TWO Big Auspicious Stars*, together with a *Golden Deity Star*. These two astrological allies of the big cat are lucky in this respect in terms of money-making prospects, although all signs can boost wealth luck with suitable activators and enhancers.

THE COLOUR FOR WEALTH: The wearing of the most auspicious colour of the spectrum RED will bring significant added benefits in 2021. Red is the colour which represents ultimate YANG, which serves to boost the year's vitality, but will do double duty in enhancing the missing Wealth element of the year. Red in 2021 stands for WEALTH, so wearing this colour as part of your wardrobe or accessories will give you a

For Wealth

boost of good fortune. You should also carry the **"Increase Your Wealth Luck" Gold Talisman Card** featuring the God of Wealth Tsai Shen Yeh seated on a Tiger. This will attract wealth of the kind that keeps increasing and will help you tap the hidden wealth luck of the year.

You can also display the **Bejewelled God of Wealth sitting on a Tiger** in figurine form in the home.

Bejewelled God of Wealth
sitting on a Tiger

Before the New Year arrives, make sure you get our specially created **Red Wealth Wallet** featuring the Wealth Ox. It is auspicious each year to change to a new wallet and especially lucky to take some money from your old wallet and transfer it over to your new wallet. Doing so for this year will ensure you take some of the energy of last year, and carry it over into the following year. In 2021 you definitely want to do this, as the previous Year of the Rat carried two *Lap Chuns*, or two "Springs" while this year has none.

Keep the lights in your home brightly turned on throughout the year, especially in the WEST sector, which plays host to the Prosperity Star #8.

POWERFUL SPIRITUAL ENHANCER: For Wealth Luck that is potent and long-lasting, an excellent ritual to incorporate into your life is the **White Dzambala Ritual**. Invite in **White Dzambala and the Four Dakinis** who pull in

wealth from the four directions. Display in a respectful place in the home and recite White Dzambala's mantra as regularly as you can.

White Dzambala's Mantra:
Om Padma Krodha Arya Dzambala Hridaya Hum Phat

When you gaze upon him and chant his mantra regularly, he manifests great riches in your life and attracts incredible opportunities that can bring wealth of a big meaningful and lasting kind.

INVITE IN THE ROOSTER: The Rooster brings the #8 Wealth Star in 2021, so it is extremely auspicious to have many images of Roosters in the home this year. The Rooster is also the symbol that ensures politicking is kept to a minimum, protecting against harmful gossip and slander. The Rooster is also wonderful for protecting the marriage, preventing any troublesome third party from trying to come between husband and wife.

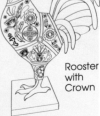

Rooster with Crown

There are many benefits to displaying the Rooster this year; indeed, it may be a good time to start collecting Roosters, made of different colours and in different materials if you wish. You can also display Rooster Art in the home, which is most auspicious. Display in the West part of the home.

Our new **Rooster with Crown** this year has been embellished with powerful symbols of protection and good fortune, to ensure the negative energies of the year cannot harm you. It features the "Anti Evil-Eye" to protect against jealousy, the Double Dorje for wisdom in decision making and the powerful "Hum" seed syllable for strong protection. Its powerful feathers sweep away all harmful energies and its crown symbolizes holding dominion over the year.

LUCKY SPECIAL STARS OF 2021

Sixth, there are two potentially VERY AUSPICIOUS stars in the year's Four Pillars chart. These are seriously good stars noted for being strong and very explicit in their beneficial influence. These stars have the capability of bringing incredible good fortune to those who know how to activate them correctly, while making sure the positive aspects of their influences materialize.

These stars impact different animal signs differently and in varying degrees, but are nevertheless very beneficial for all signs. Note that you will need to wear or carry the relevant activators to ensure that you make the most of the positive influence of these stars.

THE STAR OF PROSPECTS
brings many new opportunities

This star brought by the Earthly Branch of Rat in the Hour Pillar with the self-element of Water indicates many new opportunities in the coming year. This favourable star conjures up a very special energy that rewards determination and staying power, resonating

HOUR	DAY	MONTH	YEAR
壬 Yang Water	癸 Yin Water	庚 Yang Metal	辛 Yin Metal
壬子 Yang Water Rat	己未 Yin Earth Sheep	甲寅 Yang Wood Tiger	己丑 Yin Earth Ox

The Star of Prospects brings many new opportunities in the coming year.

with the Ox sign of the year, a reminder that those who retain their passion for success will benefit from its presence. This star suggests there is nothing that cannot be achieved for those prepared to work hard. The more ambitious one is, the further one can go this year.

> **STAR OF PROSPECTS**: To activate this star in your favour, keep an **image of an Ox** near you. We suggest the **Bejewelled Asset Bull** to magnify wealth luck and to ensure the hard work you put in meets with proportionate success. This bull has been designed with an auspicious saddle in red, the colour that signifies wealth in 2021, wearing a harness of coins and stepping on a pile of wealth and ingots, symbolizing the accumulation of assets.
>
> This beautiful enhancer will allow you to accumulate everything you work for and ensure you do not spend everything you earn. It will also increase the opportunities that come your way.

THE STAR OF POWERFUL MENTORS
brings Benefactor Luck

The Star of Powerful Mentors which was also in last year's chart makes another appearance in 2021. This star is brought by the OX in the Year Pillar and the Heavenly Stem of YANG METAL in the Month Pillar. This star is especially beneficial for the younger generation, who have the auspicious luck of influential people turning up in their lives to help them, giving them meaningful advice and powerful support.

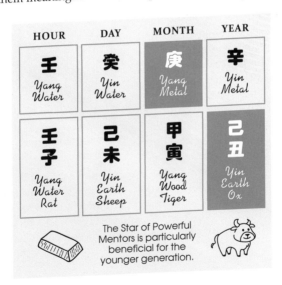

HOUR	DAY	MONTH	YEAR
壬 Yang Water	癸 Yin Water	庚 Yang Metal	辛 Yin Metal
壬子 Yang Water Rat	己未 Yin Earth Sheep	甲寅 Yang Wood Tiger	己丑 Yin Earth Ox

The Star of Powerful Mentors is particularly beneficial for the younger generation.

For students hungry for success, mentors will open doors to scholarship, and teachers will provide fabulous inspiration and motivation. Opportunities abound and there will be unseen hands supporting you. Those just starting out in your careers can find a mentor figure to guide you and to show you the ropes. An influential boss could fast-track your promotion up the ranks.

ACTIVATE THE STAR OF POWERFUL MENTORS: Bring this star to life by displaying **Kuan Kung** in the home. You can also display near to you work or study desk. Another powerful activator for this star is the **Nobleman Qui Ren Talisman**. The

benefits of this special star are immense, so it is worth activating. It brings help from the heavens, manifesting someone in your life with the wish and means to help you, and ensures those with this kind of power stay firmly on your side.

AFFLICTIVE STARS OF 2021

There are two unlucky stars brought by the Four Pillars chart of the year. These, when not attended to with relevant cures, can wreak a lot of havoc and create a lot of misfortune, but their ill influence can be avoided if you take special note and address them.

THE AGGRESSIVE SWORD STAR
is a Double-Edged Sword

The Aggressive Sword Star formed by the Yin Water in the Heavenly Stem of the Day Pillar and the Earthly Branch of Ox in the Year Pillar suggests a year of

The Aggressive Sword Star can be both good and bad.

intense aggression. It indicates the strengthening of the underdog's chi, so it points to a rise of revolutionary fervour, people revolting against authority. Strikes continue, spawning groups around the globe to walk similar paths. Protests advocating for greater equality, non-discrimination, fighting against police brutality and other social injustices continue to pick up steam. There will be anger, passion, rioting and violence.

At its pinnacle, the presence of this star suggests the emergence of powerful leaders on opposing sides, or of highly influential opposition to established leaders. It suggests the rise of a people who seize power by fair means or foul. The name of this star is *Yang Ren*, which describes "*yang essence sharp blade that inflicts damage*". This is a star with great potential for either very good or very bad influences to materialize during the year, although generally, the influence tends to be more negative than positive. There is risk of revolution and of the toppling of unpopular leaders in power.

The Aggressive Sword Star brings potential for violence & bloodshed. This star must be strongly subdued.

In this year's chart, the *Star of Aggressive Sword* is created by the strong YIN WATER of the DAY pillar, with the presence of the OX in the YEAR pillar. Here, note that the WATER element is strong in the chart, making the presence of the Aggressive Sword much more negative. It indicates that those emerging as leaders for the underdog in 2021 will end up being heavy-handed and quick-tempered. They may be charismatic but they will also be strong-willed, conceited, arrogant, overbearing and self-centered - all nasty traits that spell the potential for bloodshed and violence wherever they emerge. There is real danger of that this year!

CURE: To shield against the harmful effects of the Aggressive Sword Star, the best remedy is a powerful spiritual Stupa. The **Kumbum Stupa** is especially beneficial as it contains one hundred holy images, invoking the protection of all the world's Wisdom Protectors. This Stupa will ensure that all family members living within the home stay protected against aggression or violence of any kind. It is also a good idea to wear or carry the **28 Hums Protection Wheel Amulet** at all times.

Kumbum Stupa

THE FLOWER OF ROMANCE STAR (EXTERNAL) *makes marriages vulnerable*

This star is sometimes confused with the *Peach Blossom Star* because it addresses the destiny of love; but while both influence love and romance, they are very different in their effects. When the Flower of Romance is present, it suggests love blossoms easily, but it is not the kind of love that leads to marriage and family. It indicates instead the possibility of extramarital affairs, bringing stress and unhappiness to married couples. There is also a difference between *internal* and *external romance,* and in this year of the Ox, it is unfortunately the latter that prevails. So the year

HOUR	DAY	MONTH	YEAR
壬 Yang Water	癸 Yin Water	庚 Yang Metal	辛 Yin Metal
壬子 Yang Water Rat	己未 Yin Earth Sheep	甲寅 Yang Wood Tiger	己丑 Yin Earth Ox

The External Flower of Romance Star brings stress and risk of infidelity to marriages.

is likely to see increased occurrences of infidelity and break-ups of marriages.

Marriages are vulnerable to the External Flower of Romance this year.

The SHEEP in the Day Pillar and RAT of the Hour Pillar indicate the presence of the *External Romance Star*, making all marriages vulnerable to straying by husband OR wife. Things are made worse as the Sheep clashes with the ruling animal of the year, the Ox. This causes misunderstandings between couples, and danger of an outsider fanning the flames from the side.

FIXING THE EXTERNAL STAR OF ROMANCE: To prevent this affliction from doing real harm to your marriage, carry the **Enhancing Relationships Amulet**, especially if you suspect your spouse already has eyes for someone outside your marriage. Or if you are constantly fighting with each other, or forced into a situation when you have to spend large amounts of time apart (e.g. if one of you commutes to a different country for work, or travel a lot for work). It is also a good idea to display a pair of **Marriage Happiness Ducks** in the SW of the home, or if you suspect something has already started, place an **Amethyst Geode** tied with red string under the foot of the bed of the straying partner.

You can also invite in the **image of an Ox and Horse** to counter the affliction. This subdues the possibility of infidelity causing problems for you. The OX/HORSE presence will create a special "cross" with the SHEEP/RAT affliction.

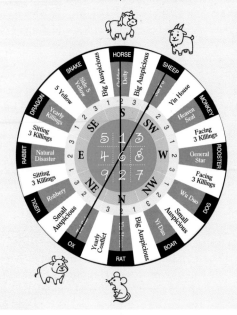

Flying Stars of 2021
Chapter 4

FLYING STAR CHART OF 2021
Heavenly Star *rules the year*

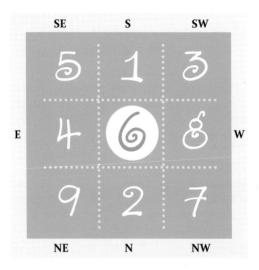

The Flying Star chart on first glance is a big improvement on last year's chart. The Loss Star #7 of 2020 makes way for the *Heaven Star* #6 in this Year of the Ox 2021. The Heaven Star becomes the dominant star of this year. This white star is associated with many good things, attracting the celestial luck of the heavens and providing the unseen hand of opportunity and guidance from above. Everyone stands to benefit from this star, especially if the center of the home where the star is located is kept well-energized and active throughout the year.

In 2021, it benefits to keep the center of the home very active! Have friends over & use this space well.

Rearrange your furniture so you naturally gravitate to the center of your home. The more you include this space in daily usage, the better the luck of the whole family for this coming year.

2021's chart suits homes with open plan layouts arranged around the center part of the home. This is where the luck of auspicious heaven energy congregates this year, and keeping this part of the home lively and vibrant with lots of music, chatter and activity will serve to "activate" this star, bringing it to life!

Work at repositioning your furniture and seating if you have to. This year it is extremely auspicious for all members of the household to spend plenty of time in the center sector, and when you have guests, entertain them in this part of the home. If your home has a piano, place it in the center so every time someone sits down to play it, the sector gets energized.

If your home is not an open-concept one, keep the doors to the center room in the home ajar as much as possible.

You want the energy that emanates from the center to seep into all other areas of the home. The more you energize this part of your house, and the more you suppress the bad luck sectors, the better the luck of the whole household for the year.

ENHANCE THE CENTER GRID
with the Celestial Water Dragon

This year, every household benefits from the presence of the **Celestial Water Dragon**. Place this celestial creature in the center of your home and of your office. The celestial Dragon is the ultimate symbol of good fortune and its deep blue colour and cloud imagery suggest its heavenly origins. This Dragon is auspicious wherever he is displayed, but this year he especially benefits the center part of the home, which houses the Heaven Star #6.

The Celestial Water Dragon is the best enhancer for the #6 Heaven Star which occupies the central sector in 2021.

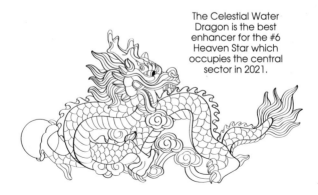

Placing the Celestial Water Dragon here attracts plenty of new and lucrative opportunities into your life, as well as the patrons, mentors and contacts you need to support you in whatever path you choose to take. Individuals and organizations in a position to help you and open doors for you will somehow find their way into your life. The presence of the Celestial Dragon always attracts abundance and success, and this year, inviting in this Dragon brings a very special kind of good fortune indeed.

Invoking the power of THE EIGHT IMMORTALS

Another excellent energizer for the center is the **8 Celestial Immortals Plaque**. The 8 Immortals bring eight kinds of good fortune and protects against harm. In Chinese mythology, they are a revered group of legendary beings each with a unique talent or ability.

Place the 8 Immortals Plaque in the center of the home in 2021.

These eight saints have been depicted in Chinese art since time immemorial as they are believed to bestow wealth, longevity and spiritual awakening on all who glance upon them.

Depicted as a group, they bring a balanced basket of good fortune and protection for the whole family. They hail from the 8 different compass directions and are usually shown with their unique symbols representing the luck each brings.

Zhang Guo Lao, protector of the North, **brings the luck of good descendants**. His symbol is the bamboo flute and his element is Water. He enjoys drinking wine and is famous for making his own which had curative and healing powers. He is said to be able to drink poison without harm and offers protection against the dark arts. He is often shown with his companion, the mule.

Chao Guo Jiu, protector of the Northeast, **brings the luck of control**. He is excellent for those in positions of authority who have to motivate and retain the support of those they command. His element is Earth and his symbol are the castanets. According to legend, he went to great lengths to avoid casualties of war, protecting the innocent from harm during battle. He is skilled in the magical arts and possesses great wisdom and charisma to lead with great authority.

Lee Dong Bin, protector of the West, **brings protection against evil**. His element is Metal and his implement is the Magic Sword. He is famed for being a great scholar and poet, and for his exceptional intelligence. While he had certain character flaws – he was a serial womanizer - he was known for his dedication to helping others elevate their spiritual growth.

He Xian Gu, protector of the Southwest, **bestows family and marriage luck**. Her element is Earth and her symbol is the Lotus Blossom. The only lady among the 8, she has also grown to become a symbol of woman power. She is often accompanied by a mythical bird said to reign over all birds, bringing new opportunities from near and far. She helps stabilize married couples, protecting the sacred sanctity of marriage and bestowing a happy family life. She protects against troublemakers who threaten to break up happy families. For those who are single, she is said to attract marriage opportunities and suitable suitors.

Han Xiang Zi, protector of the Southeast, **brings healing energies** to those who are sick, but more particularly, he helps heal those with a broken heart. His element is Wood and his symbol is the flute. His legendary past involves the tragic love story where he fell in love with the daughter of the Dragon King, who did not grant the couple his blessings. Theirs was a star-crossed romance without a happy ending, but the bamboo flute he wields was said to be a gift from his beloved. Playing on his flute healed him emotionally, and from there on he vowed to help others the same way.

Lan Chai He, protector of the Northwest, **brings scholastic and creative luck**. His element is Metal and his symbol the flower basket. He is often shown with his swan, symbolic of his lyrical gifts. He is said to have become immortal when the Monkey King bestowed 500 years of magic upon him. His companion is the Monkey. As well as his flair for the arts, he is said to possess a sharp intelligence and wit.

Han Zhong Li, protector of the East, **brings longevity and wealth**. His element is Wood and his symbols are the magical fan and peach. His fan is said to have the ability to heal the sick, even bring the dead back to life, as well as turning stones to silver and gold. His peach is the fruit of immortality which grants a long life filled with happiness.

Tie Guai Lee, protector of the South, **brings wisdom and healing**. His element is Fire and his symbol is the Bottle Gourd. He is often depicted as an unkempt old man with disheveled hair, taking on the appearance of a beggar. His chosen role is to care for those who are sick, poor or in need.

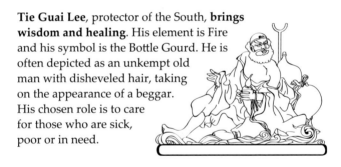

Enhance for Future Prosperity
in the Northeast

The animal sign of the year, the Ox plays host to the *Future Prosperity Star #9*. This star signifies imminent wealth just about to ripen, and the closer we get to Period 9, which starts Feb 4th 2024, the shorter the waiting time for what is considered "future wealth". The #9 is also a magnifying star, which gains power as we head into Period 9. The Ox sign this year thus gets energized with the presence of this star in its sector. The NE is also the place of the Tiger, who features as always in the year's Paht Chee in the month pillar.

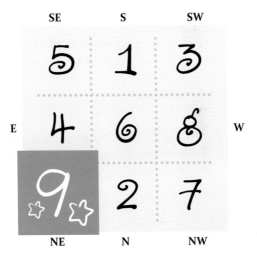

SE	S	SW
5	1	3
4	6	8
9 ⭐⭐	2	7
NE	**N**	**NW**

The NE plays host to the "Future Prosperity Star"

The powerful Fire star #9 brings vitality to all who come under its influence, and its presence in the ruling animal sector bodes well for the coming year. This star benefits homes that face NE, and individuals whose bedrooms or office rooms are located NE, as well as those born under the signs of Ox and Tiger.

The #9 in the NE suggests that the central #6 heavenly star gets strengthened. This is a lucky star for most of the year, except for months when monthly flying stars here are unfavourable – i.e. March, May, July, August and December 2021. When unfavourable monthly stars visit, ensure you have the relevant cures in place and keep this sector less active during these times.

ENHANCERS FOR THE NORTHEAST

The NE benefits from the **9 Golden Dragons Plaque** featuring nine celestial Dragons that bestow power and generates the capacity to pursue all one's grandest ambitions conviction and courage.

Having nine Dragons in the NE allows you to stay focused on long-term goals without getting distracted,

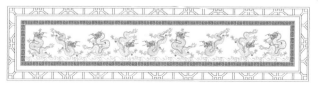

Display the 9 Golden Dragons Plaque in the NE.

or discouraged by short-term difficulties. They protect you against those who wish to see you fail, and shields you from the effects of less ambitious relatives or acquaintances who do not have your vision.

Displaying this plaque in the NE of your home or office ensures you have the support of not one but *nine* Dragons, the number that symbolizes completion and abundance. The number 9 is a magical number as it is a number that always reduces back to itself when multiplied. It also strengthens the #9 star, which is getting stronger as we move rapidly towards a fast-approaching Period of 9.

BUILD YOUR WEALTH: You should also activate the NE with a collection of **Wealth Cabinets**. These wealth cabinets symbolize an accumulation of asset wealth, meaning that the money you make accrues into ever-larger amounts that can last into the many generations. Energizing the NE helps you to make enough money so you do not have to spend everything you earn. It allows you to grow wealthy enough to carve out a secure, comfortable and worry-free future for yourself and your loved ones.

Activate for Love & Romance
in the EAST

The Peach Blossom Star #4 settles into in the East sector this year. This star gets greatly enhanced in 2021 as the East is the place of the Rabbit, the creature associated with the Moon, and with the Goddess of the Moon who governs all fortunes to do with love, romance and relationships. Legend has it that when you catch the attention of the Moon Goddess, she aids you in all matters related to the heart, improving relations between lovers and even matchmaking those who are destined to be together.

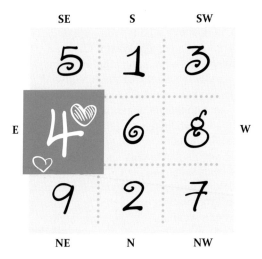

The East plays host to the Peach Blossom Star,
which brings romance.

For those who are single, activating this sector with the **Rabbit in the Moon** awakens the powers of **Moon Goddess**, alerting her to all wishes to do with affairs of the heart. Enhancing this sector promotes the success of relationships, attracts marriage opportunities, smooths interactions between spouses, and imbues stale marriages with a newfound passion and vigour.

The EAST becomes the place of the MOON RABBIT in 2021, harnessing the power of the Lunar Mansions to bring great love and romance into the lives of those who activate this luck.

This is the sector to enhance if love is what you are looking for! This year we have designed the **Rabbit in the Moon**, the earthly messenger of this lunar goddess. Placing this activator in the East will help singles meet their soulmates and forever partners, while helping those who are already married to keep their spouses. Remember that this year's Paht Chee generates the unfavourable *External Flower of Romance Star*, which can cause problems within already existing relationships, resulting in unwanted love triangles and other outside disturbances to a love relationship. Invoking the blessings of the **Rabbit in the Moon** ensures that only the positive aspects of love materialize. It will also protect against unpleasantness associated with matters of the heart. They say there is nothing sweeter than love, but they also say that nothing breaks like a heart – remember the song by Mark Ronson and Miley Cyrus? Heartache and heartbreak can be far more painful than physical pain; the #4 in the East brings the Moon Rabbit to life and provides a solution for those looking for happiness in love.

ATTRACTING MARRIAGE OPPORTUNITIES

For those looking for a soul mate, someone you can settle down with and make a future with, or if you are already dating but your partner seems a long way off from proposing marriage, you can speed things along with the help of your **Peach Blossom Animal**. Our new Peach Blossom animals the **Rat**, **Rabbit**, **Horse** and **Rooster** come with trees of fortune enhanced with potent symbols of love and marriage. The **Peach Blossom Rooster** brings love and marriage opportunities to the **Rat**, **Dragon** and **Monkey**. If you are looking for love that leads to marriage or would like your current partner to propose, display a **Peach Blossom Rooster** in the WEST, or in the EAST in 2021.

Peach Blossom Rooster

For students,
activate the Scholastic Star in the EAST

For young people and anyone pursuing their studies, engaged in research or in search of new knowledge, they can activate the scholastic star of the year which flies to the East in 2021. The #4 is also the star number that brings study and exam luck; when properly activated, it has the power to help you achieve success in anything related to scholastic accolades. Enhancing this star improves clarity of mind, allowing you to absorb new knowledge and to process it with much greater efficiency. Anything requiring cognitive

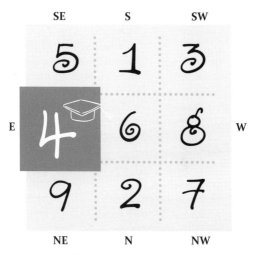

The #4 star in the East is also the Star of Scholarship

reasoning and abilities gets enhanced when you harness the energies of this star number.

The #4 Scholastic Star also boosts creativity and original thinking, allowing you to better come up with unique and innovative new ideas. This star gets strengthened this year, as it is a Wood star flying into a Wood sector.

ENHANCE THE SCHOLASTIC STAR: The best way to activate the #4 for scholastic luck is to carry **Manjushri's Gau**. Manjushri is the Buddha of Wisdom, and when you call on his help, he slices through your ignorance so only wisdom remains. His flaming sword removes all that is obscured in your mind, allowing you to think with a clear head so you can map out effective solutions to everything you are pursuing.

For students taking exams, having Manjushri's support enables them to recall everything they have revised and studied, and to write excellent answers in their exam. Manjushri boosts everything to do with wisdom and intelligence, and helps one to make wise choices. He ensures one constantly sees the big picture, while also filling in the details. For school-going children, they can clip **Manjushri's Amulet** onto their schoolbag. The specially-designed **Scholastic Amulet with Manjushri's mantra** sums up all of his wisdom and blessings, providing an endless stream of support, reinforcement and inspiration.

FOR EXAM LUCK:

For students taking important exams and hoping to do well, there is no better enhancer than the **Dragon Carp**. The carp that jumps over the Dragon Gate and successfully transforms into a Dragon is the best symbol of success for anyone aspiring to scholastic success. It promotes the luck of the scholarship and helps students not just pass exams but excel in them. The Dragon Carp also generates a strong sense of self-motivation, ensuring one does not fall into bad company or get side-tracked into unproductive tasks. This is the best enhancer for children or teenagers looking to perform well in important exams, to win awards, to gain scholarships and grants and to gain admission into colleges of their choice.

The academic path of today is filled with potholes and pitfalls, far more than in the old days, as everything has become so much more competitive. More and more young people are fighting for fewer places at top universitie and colleges; at school, children are faced with competition from classmates with Tiger parents in the sidelines egging them on. For a young mind, it can all become too much, and with all the expectations heaped on young shoulders these days, sometimes all it takes is one bad test or one bad result to cause a child to throw in the towel and just give up.

As parents, we need to imbue in our children not just the impetus to keep striving for the top, but help them understand there will be bumps and disappointments along the way. It is not necessary to perform every single day of the year, to come out top in every single test; what is important is to peak when it counts. The **Dragon Carp** stabilizes one's mind, helping a child along the academic path navigate all that comes his or her way with a strong and mature mind, resulting in success when it truly matters.

Transform Five Yellow Misfortune Star
in the Southeast

The bogus star, the Five Yellow, makes its way into the Southeast this year. The good news is that because the Southeast is a Wood Sector, it mitigates the extent of damage of this dangerous Earth star, as Wood destroys Earth in the cycle of elements. When the Five Yellow flies into a Wood sector, misfortune can be turned into opportunity. This is why we have designed this year's **Five Element Pagoda with a Tree of Life**. This alters the effects of the *wu wang*, suppressing the darker side of this star while

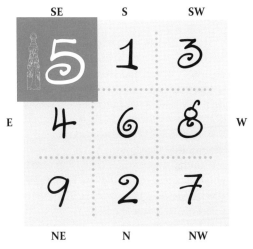

The 5 Yellow afflicts the SE in 2021 but with the correct cure, this Five Yellow has the potential to bring great good luck!

harnessing its benevolent powers. This star affects those living in homes that face SE, those with bedrooms or work rooms in the SE, and those born in years of the Dragon and Snake.

If your house has more than one level, make sure you have a **Five Element Pagoda with Tree of Life** on every floor. Keep the SE of the home free from too much activity and noise, and avoid renovations in this part of the home in 2021. Whatever you do, DO NOT renovate the SE of the home this year.

Victory Star brings winning luck
to the South

The White Star #1 associated with victory and winning luck makes its way to the South. This star allows you to triumph in any situation and to attain success over any competition you may face. In 2021, this star benefits those whose bedrooms are located South, and all those living in homes that face South. Anyone who spends a lot of time in this part of their home can also tap into the good luck this star brings by keeping it well energized with the correct activators. The livelier you keep this part of the home, the better!

The Victory Star this year is made more potent as it is supported by not one but **TWO Big Auspicious**

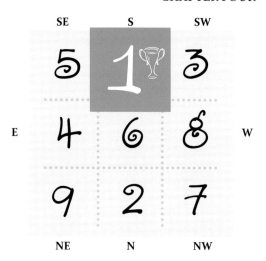

The South sector enjoys the Victory Star in 2021.

Stars from the 24 Mountains, as well as the **Golden Deity Star**, echoing the benefits of the ruling star of the year, the #6 Heaven Star. All this serves to increase the power and effectiveness of this star, so it is really worthwhile to actively enhance this star. Because the South is the sector governing the reputation of the household, the #1 here also improves one's standing and repute in various circles – work, social, etc.

ACTIVATE THE VICTORY STAR:
The best enhancer for the Victory Star is the
Victorious Windhorse Carrying a Jewel. The
Windhorse is the very essence of success luck,
known as the magical steed of the folk hero
King Gesar, who when riding his Windhorse
could never be defeated. His horse with flaming
red coat has become synonymous with success
and victory, and his image is what is needed
whenever one needs to boost one's chances
against others in any kind of competitive
situation. In 2021, we recommend everyone to
place the Victorious Windhorse in the South.
This sector is also the home sector of the Horse,
an auspicious creature that emanates pure
Fire energy. Displaying images and figurines
of horses in general in the South is thus very
appropriate and auspicious indeed.

Activate the
#1 Star in the
South with
the Victorious
Windhorse
Carrying a
Jewel.

BOOST POWER AND AUTHORITY:
For those in positions of leadership and management, the best way to enhance your effectiveness as a leader is with the help of the **Ru Yi**. The Ru Yi is the royal scepter of power, which bestows "the right to rule". In ancient China, anyone in any kind of power would never be seen without a Ru Yi at his side. You can place your Ru Yi in front of you on your work desk, or carry in your bag.

The **Crimson Red Ru Yi with Bats** brings the luck of **success and abundance**. Any boss, head or leader can use the help of this Ru Yi to ensure things between all in their group stay harmonious, joyful and productive at all times. It attracts the luck of abundance and success, so whatever is pursued turns out fruitful and effective. It helps you to ensure all your final goals are reached in the most harmonious way.

Anyone in any kind of leadership position needs a Ru Yi.

The **Deep Blue Ru Yi with 8 Auspicious Symbols** brings the luck of **wealth**. This Ru Yi includes the Victory Banner for winning luck, the Double Fish for abundance, the Parasol for protection, the Conch for good news, the Wheel for sustainability, the Mystic Knot for longevity, the Vase for completion and the Lotus for good intentions.

These symbols of good fortune are the magical implements of the Eight Immortals, and act as vessels of their power. Carrying images of their magical symbols on a Ru Yi imbues you with a complete collection of the different kinds of luck you need to reach your full potential as a leader.

The **Yellow Ru Yi with Celestial Dragon** brings the luck of **power and position**. Those operating in political environments or in politics need this Ru Yi! It bestows charisma and magnetism, and endows strength to make your position one that is stable and secure. It ensures you do not get plotted against and overthrown. It protects against betrayal and treachery and gives you power over those on the outside as well as on the inside.

The SOUTH is the place to activate if success, victory, fame and reputation is what you seek.

Suppress the Quarrelsome Star
in the Southwest

The Quarrelsome Star #3 flies to the Southwest, bringing hostile energy and complications associated with arguments, misunderstandings and court cases. The #3 star can also cause serious aggravations that lead to violence and tragedy. This affliction affects anyone with a bedroom in the SW, those whose main doors face SW, and those born in years of the Sheep and Monkey. It also affects the Matriarch of the household. The #3 star is especially strong this year,

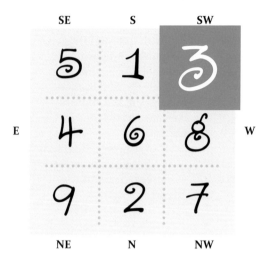

Beware the #3 quarrelsome star in the SW this year.

as the intrinsic Wood energy of the star dominates the Earth energy of the SW. The effects of this star are made worse as the SW also plays host to the **Yin House** from the 24 Mountains. All this suggests that this affliction MUST be taken seriously.

Anything that suggests Fire is an effective cure, so keeping the lights turned on brightly in this sector will help combat the negative energies of this star. **The colour red** is also suitable, so red curtains, rugs and cushion covers here will help very much indeed.

CURES FOR THE QUARRELSOME STAR:
For 2021, the best remedy for the Quarrelsome Star in the SW is the **Nine Phoenix Plaque** in red and gold. These celestial birds in red and gold - which represent the elements of Fire and Metal - work to subdue this troublesome Wood Star. The Fire energy engulfs the Wood of the #3, while the Metal energy of the gold effectively subdues it.

The Nine Phoenix Plaque is an excellent cure against the #3 Quarrelsome Star.

We also recommend placing **red carpets** in this sector, or in the SW portion of any room you spend a lot of time in. Another effective cure for the #3 are the **Red Peace and Harmony Apples**. In Chinese, the word for peaceful is *Ping*, which sounds like the word for apple – *Ping Kor*. This year's Peace Apples comes embossed with the English word "Peace" and the Chinese rhyming couplet carrying the meaning "If your intentions are good and your heart is pure, the world will be peaceful."

124

Place this pair of apples in the SW to ensure all members of the household stay supportive of one another, and to prevent clashes and conflict from arising. Also an excellent cure for use within the office to maintain a productive and supportive environment between colleagues and workmates.

Enhance Prosperity Star 8 *in the West*

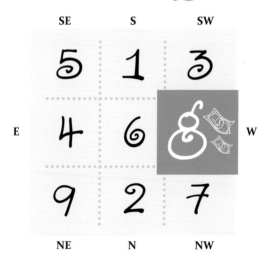

The Wealth Star #8 flies to the West this year.

The very lucky Wealth Star #8 makes its way to the West, the sector of the Rooster. This star is also known as the *Current Prosperity Star*, as we are currently in the Period of 8. The West is the sector that represents children and descendants, suggesting that the wealth this sector brings will last into the long term, reaching future generations and for many generations to come. It points to a successful accumulation of assets over time if properly energized.

In 2021, the West can be considered one of the luckiest areas of the home, because it enjoys this auspicious #8 star. The strong energy of the current period emanating from this sector benefits all homes whose main entrances face West, and all bedrooms and offices located in the West benefit from this luck. The West is also the place of the youngest daughter, so the wealth this sector brings benefits the young girls of the house.

WEALTH luck takes root in the WEST sector this year so this is the area of the home you should enhance for greater prosperity luck.

Remember that to activate the luck of this auspicious star #8, the West should be thoroughly imbued with yang energy - this means lots of activity, lots of noise and plenty of bright lights. When there is movement, sound, chatter and merry-making, the number 8 comes to life, bringing good fortune and big prosperity. In the constellations, 8 is a "man-made star" with two assistants – on the right and on the left - so that at its strongest moments, it brings wealth and great nobility.

When the 8 can turn dangerous...
Beware however. The number becomes negative when afflicted by structures in the environment that threaten its location. If the West sector of your home has too much Metal energy, or if there are harmful physical structures that cause poison arrows to direct threatening energy your way, that is when the number 8 can bring harm to young children especially young daughters of the household, causing illness to arise. If there are such structures external to your home, but towards the West, it is important to block the view

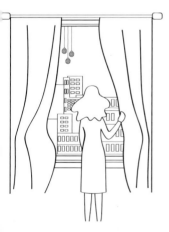

with curtains, or dissipate the killing energy with **facetted crystal balls**. These will disperse the worst of the killing breath before it has the chance to enter your home.

If the view from your window to the WEST is of a threatening looking building with sharp edges or poison arrows, keep the curtains in this area closed to block the offending view from spoiling your feng shui. Hang facetted crystal balls here.

ACTIVATE FOR WEALTH IN THE WEST

The best way to manifest wealth luck in 2021 is the make sure the West part of your home is well-energized with wealth symbols. Because this is the year of the Ox, this creature is especially lucky as it symbolizes harnessing the good fortune of the year. Because the West represents children and descendants, this prosperity luck benefits the whole family not just in the present but into the long term.

The image of the Ox has great power to attract abundant good fortune in 2021. Displaying images of the Ox in all sizes and permutations is so lucky this year! For the collectors among you, a good time to start "collecting" Ox images.

A fabulous wealth enhancer for this year is the **Asset Wealth Bull**. This Bull holds the symbolic and subliminal message "May the market bull for you"! With resplendent red saddle and surrounded by coins, ingots and symbols of prosperity, this bull energizes for wealth of the kind that can accumulate into expanded net worth, the kind that provides meaningful disposable income, providing a worry-free future.

Display the Asset Wealth Bull for wealth that grows and expands your net worth!

To tap the hidden wealth of the year, display the **Ox finding Hidden Wealth**. This Ox is depicting calmly and unobtrusively grazing in a field full of coins, sniffing out hidden wealth and opportunities. In a year with little obvious wealth but a lot of hidden wealth, this Ox generates the luck that allows you to tap the full potential of the year.

Invite in the "Ox Finding Hidden Wealth" to tap the full potential of the year.

Another great activator for this year's wealth star is the **Tree Bringing 3 Kinds of Wealth**.

Trees always depict growth energy, and when they look like money trees, they really do bring the luck of wealth into the home! Our tree this year has been designed to represent the manifestation of 3 different kinds of wealth - Asset Wealth, Income Wealth and Growth Wealth. Having all three kinds of wealth brings you not just enough to lead a comfortable life now, it gives you security and peace of mind and allows you to plan for the future. This year's wealth tree also features 12 lucky charms to signify abundance in all forms entering your life- the Double Fish, the Apple, the Treasure Chest, the Golden Ingot, the Wealth Vase, the Abacus, the I-Ching Coin, Gold bars, the 4-leafed clover the Maneki Neko Lucky Cat and the Pot of Gold.

This year's wealth tree represents not just prosperity luck but also the luck of asset accumulation. This symbolises your wealth growing and your networth expanding.

Beware Betrayal & Loss Star
in the Northwest

A dangerous aspect of this year's chart is the #7 Robbery Star in the NW. This brings loss and betrayal energies to the Patriarch, which not only means the patriarch of the family, but leaders, bosses, managers and anyone responsible for the welfare or livelihood of others. The presence of the #7 in the NW suggests that the Patriarch could get cheated, conned or betrayed. It brings the energy that suggests you should keep your friends close but your enemies closer.

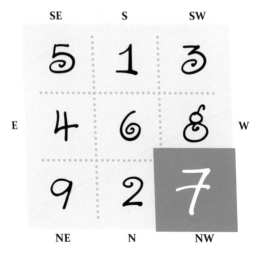

The NW, the sector of the Patriarch and Leader, gets afflicted by the #7 Loss and Betrayal Star in 2021.

In 2021, keep your friends close but your enemies closer!

Stay alert like a hawk, as treachery can strike at any moment. The energies of the year could corrupt even the most trustworthy of friends and the most loyal of employees. The #7 Robbery Star, like its namesake, describes a situation when you are cheated out of money; but it can also manifest as an actual robbery. We recommend all who stay out late, or who venture anywhere even remotely unsafe, to carry the **Nightspot Protection Amulet**. Because this star affects the NW, it harms the Father the most, but there can be knock-on adverse effects on the rest of the family, or the rest of a leader's charges.

CURE FOR #7 STAR: This year the best cure for the #7 star in the home is the **Anti-Burglary Plaque with Door Guardians**. These Door Gods with spear in the ready are depicted with the Anti-Burglary Amulets, with the Chinese proverb, "May your family be blessed with peace, safety and abundant joy, may your home be filled with everlasting happiness."

Display in the NW to ensure your home stays protected against unexpected and unwanted intruders, who may cause not just loss of property and possessions, but loss of peace of mind. These door guardians will help keep your family protected through the year.

BEWARE BETRAYAL:

This year, risk of betrayal is rife as the #7 star occupies the NW, the location of the leader. Betrayal means duplicity from those you trust, those you least suspect and therefore those you are most vulnerable to. While it feels nasty to get cheated by conmen and people you do not know, when betrayals come from those closest to you, the harm is emotional as well as physical. The loss is no longer merely monetary, it hits a nerve deep within that can be difficult to take and recover from. This year, because opportunity for this to happen gets increased, we suggest to remove temptation where you can, watch your back, and carry symbols to protect against this kind of bad luck. Carry the **Kuan Kung Anti-Betrayal Amulet**. This specially-designed talisman features the amulet that protects against being stabbed in the back, with the mantra that ensures the protection is effective.

Kuan Kung on horseback
Anti-Betrayal Amulet

PROTECT AGAINST BEING CHEATED:
For those engaging in high-risk deals carry the **Anti-Cheating Amulet** to ensure you do not get conned by unscrupulous people. An excellent amulet for business people and for anyone dealing with new acquaintances who maybe be untrustworthy.

PROTECTION AGAINST THE DARK ARTS:
Another form of harm can come from those who practice black magic. Especially in the East, such arts are more common than you think. Even if you do not subscribe or "believe" in this kind of power, it exists. Someone who projects negative thoughts against you, whether out of spite, jealousy or some other reason, does not even have to be skilled in these methods to send negative hexes and projectiles your way!

For example, if someone curses you on the street because they are angry at the way you drive, this can result in the same kind of misfortune effect as someone actively plotting or using black magic against you. The latter is of course more serious, but whenever one is weak in terms of spirit essence and element luck, they can succumb badly when someone forms negative thoughts and sends those thoughts their way.

The best protection against this kind of harm is the **28 Hums Protection Wheel**, which features the powerful **Heart Sutra** on the back. These sacred syllables together with this powerful sutra ensures that whatever projectiles are sent your way cannot reach you. A vital cure for anyone with enemies, who are engaged in high stakes deals, or anyone who may have offended someone intentionally or unintentionally.

28 Hums
Protection
Wheel

Suppress Illness Star
in the North

The #2 Illness Star flies to the North, and because North is of the Water element, it cannot do anything on its own to weaken the energies of the #2, an Earth star. The Illness Star is further strengthened as it is supported by the **Yin House Star** in North 2, the sector of the Rat. This boosts the potency of this star, making the North sector dangerous for those who are elderly, frail or prone to illness.

It is important for anyone whose bedroom is facing North, or whose home faces North to suppress the Illness Star with strong cures.

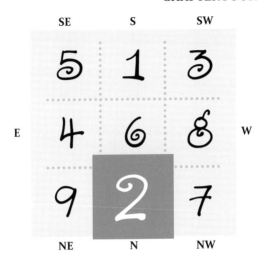

The North gets afflicted by the Illness Star this year.

CURE FOR THE ILLNESS STAR:
In 2021, a good cure for the Illness Star is the **Healing Deer Carrying Vase of Longevity with Linzhi**. The deer is renowned by the Chinese for their powerful curative properties and is often seen as the companion of the God of Longevity, Sau Seng Kong. With the world caught up in fears of epidemics and pandemics where there seems no escape with a proper cure a long time coming, the

Healing Deer

deer is an excellent shield against this kind of illness. Display in the North of the home this year. The Healing Deer is an excellent symbol of good health in the year 2021.

Another potent cure against the Illness Star #2 is the **Medicine Buddha and 7 Sugatas Gau**. Medicine Buddha always comes to the aid of those who are suffering when one calls for his help. His area of expertise is in the removal of poisons, disease and illness, and the **Medicine Buddha and 7 Sugatas Gau** features all 8 of his emanations, and his powerful mantras in whole. You can place in the North of the home to stay under his protection constantly. Excellent for anyone who is ill or feeling unwell.

You can also chant his mantra daily:
TADYATHA OM BHEKHANDZYE BHEKHANDZYE MAHA BHEKHANDZYE (BHEKHANDZYE) RADZA SAMUGATE SOHA

For those suffering from a chronic ailment, we suggest that you get yourself a dedicated **Medicine Buddha Mala** to chant with. The more you chant his mantra over the mala, the more powerful the mala will become. Keep the mala with you always, and whenever you have spare time, bring it out and chant. You can also wear the mala as an accessory around your wrist or neck.

HEART MANTRA
OF ARYA VAIROCHANA
WOFS™

AGAINST COVID-19: To protect against the coronavirus specifically, the best cure is to invite in an image of the **Buddha Vairocana**, who brings blessings of good health but also provides strong protection against contagious diseases. Display his image as a figurine, and also carry his image in the form of a **Gold Talisman Card** which we have made available to help tide us through these challenging times.

AFFLICTIONS OF 2021
TAI SUI *in the* NORTHEAST

The TAI SUI or God of the Year always occupies the sector of the ruling animal sign of the year. This year, he occupies the palace of the Ox, Northeast 1. The Tai Sui is the celestial force that governs all that happens on Earth, and when one has his support and blessings, very little can go wrong, but when one offends him, his wrath knows no bounds.

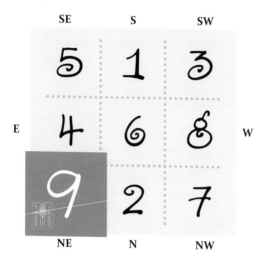

	SE	S	SW
E	5	1	3
	4	6	8	W
	9	2	7
	NE	N	NW

The Tai Sui resides in the NE this year, and it is important to keep him on your side. Place the Tai Sui Plaque 2021 here.

It is a matter of course and tradition for most Chinese who believe, to offer prayers to Tai Sui at the start of the year, humbly asking for his help and support for the coming year. In feng shui, the creature that is known to appease him is the celestial chimera the **Dragon Pi Xie**, so we always recommend to place this in the location of the Tai Sui.

The Dragon Pi Xie is said to appease the Tai Sui. Place in the NE in 2021.

PROTECTION: What is even more important is to place the **Tai Sui Plaque** with his image and invocation as a sign of respect. In 2021, place this in the NE1 sector. Animal signs especially affected by the Tai Sui this year are the Earth

signs of Sheep, Dragon and Dog, while the Ox whose location he occupies should also be mindful of his presence there. For these 4 signs, we also recommend carrying the **Tai Sui Amulet** at all times throughout the year.

THREE KILLINGS in the EAST

This affliction is said to bring three types of misfortune – loss of wealth, loss of reputation and loss of a loved one. All three are devastating, and when not one but three forms of bad luck hit you at once, the loss can be difficult and extremely distressing. This is another affliction that is important to take note of and to cure.

Firstly, NEVER have your back to the Three Killings affliction, so in 2021, DO NOT SIT FACING WEST,

EVEN if WEST is your best direction! Do not sit with your back to the East, as the Three Killings is the kind of affliction that stabs you in the back, when you are least suspecting. It carries the characteristic of hitting you when you are most comfortable and least aware. When things are at their calmest, beware, because the storm is about to pound and crash down...

NEVER HAVE YOUR BACK TO THE EAST this year! Make sure you do not get stabbed by the dangerous 3 Killings affliction!

CURE FOR THE THREE KILLINGS: Place the **3 Celestial Shields** to combat the Three Killings.

These shields act as effective armour sheltering you from the effects of this difficult affliction. All homes should display these shields in the EAST of the home in 2021. Anyone with something to lose, who operate where stakes are high, or who are going through years of low element luck are also recommended to carry the **3 Celestial Shields Amulet** when on the go. Use as a keychain or bag decoration.

Compatibilities with other Signs in 2021

Chapter 5

Dragon has to try harder when it comes to relationships

The Dragon in 2021 is afflicted by the Five Yellow, causing you to lack energy. You have little inclination to do much romancing this year, so it will be those who actively pursue you who are able to "catch" you. You continue to exude your signature charm, but when you pique someone's interest, you may exhibit some bothersome self-destructive tendencies. When things are going well, you tend to say the wrong things, setting you back several steps. Don't sabotage yourself like that! Playing the dating game may feel heavy-going this year, so it will be partners who put you at ease that can successfully win your heart.

Many different influences come into play each year to determine how one animal sign gets along with another. Chinese astrology has so many permutations that it is difficult to take note of everything, but examining some of the main variables can give useful insights to the general mood and compatibility between any two signs in any year. The annual energies of the year have a larger bearing on the effect on your relationships than you may be aware of, and understanding these effects allows you to be more effective in all your interactions.

When you find the keys to unlock what makes your connections tick, not only will this help with your happiness levels, it also improves your productivity and success potential.

Every animal sign under the Chinese Zodiac system has certain signs they are naturally drawn towards; certain signs will make better spouses, others make more exciting lovers, others still work better when you remain platonic friends. Certain pairings thrive in a business relationship, as boss and employee, mentor and mentee; others work well as parent and child, siblings, sporting teammates or drinking buddies; while others still, have the potential to change your life in a big way.

There are also certain signs you need to stay alert to and be wary of. One's Zodiac Adversary is the animal sign born six years apart from you, the sign directly opposite you in the Zodiac wheel – but in certain years, your "natural enemy" can become a useful ally, while in others, you would be best advised to stay well clear of each other. Having knowledge of how the year's energies influence your relationships will give you the edge when it comes to how you relate to others in any given year.

In this section, we analyse the relationship between the Dragon and the other signs of the Zodiac, looking in particular at the quality and nature of the relationships as determined by the influences of 2021.

1. Alliance of Allies

There are four affinity groupings that form natural allies in the horoscope. The three signs in each group have similar thought processes, aspirations and goals. Their attitudes are alike, and their support of each other is immediate and instinctive. If there is an alliance within a family unit amongst siblings, or between spouses and their child, the family is incredibly supportive, giving strength to each other. In good years, auspicious luck gets multiplied.

Astrological allies always get along. Any falling out is temporary. They trust each other and close ranks against external threats. Good astrological feng shui comes from carrying the image of your allies, especially when they are going through good years.

ALLY GROUPINGS	ANIMALS	CHARACTERISTICS
Competitors	Rat, Dragon, Monkey	Competent, Tough, Resolute
Intellectuals	Ox, Snake, Rooster	Generous, Focused, Resilient
Enthusiasts	Dog, Tiger, Horse	Aggressive, Rebellious, Coy
Diplomats	Boar, Sheep, Rabbit	Creative, Kind, Emotional

When all three signs in a particular year has good fortune, the alliance is strengthened. But in years when one sign stands out with superior luck, the others in its grouping can "lean" on that sign to lift itself up. The Dragon belongs to the grouping of Competitors in the Zodiac, comprising the Rat, Dragon and Monkey.

This year, the strongest link in the Dragon's alliance of allies is the Monkey, who has the most promising element luck in the group. For the Dragon, friends born in the year of the Monkey become a very good influence on you, and bring you good fortune luck.

In 2021, the Dragon can lean on the Monkey to gain strength. It favours the Dragon to fraternize with friends born in the year of the Monkey, who enjoy the *Heaven Seal* and bring new opportunities and breaks to its pal the Dragon. The excellent element luck of your friend the Monkey also gives you a boost of confidence and creativity.

If you do not have close friends or alliances born in the year of the Monkey, you can simulate this luck by displaying images or figurines of the Monkey in your home. Hang beautiful and inspiring art of the Monkey in your home, or display auspicious Monkey depictions. One of our favourites is the Monkey sitting on a Horse, or sitting on an elephant - this creates the luck of career success and promotion, so if this is part of your list of aspirations, this becomes especially lucky for you in 2021.

For the Dragon, displaying images of the Monkey in your living space brings you tremendous good fortune in 2021.

2. Zodiac Soulmates

Another natural ally for you is your Zodiac soulmate.In Chinese astrology, there are six pairs of signs that create six Zodiac Houses of yin and yang soulmates. Each pair creates powerful bonding on a cosmic level. Marriages or business unions between people belonging to the same Zodiac House are extremely auspicious. In a marriage, there is great love and devotion, and in a commercial partnership, it promises much wealth and success. Such a pairing is also good between professional colleagues or between siblings.

The strength of each pair is different, each having a defining strength with some making better commercial than marriage partners. How successful you are as a pair depends on how you bond. The table on the following page summarizes the key strength of each Zodiac house.

For the Dragon, your Zodiac Soulmate is the Snake. Together you form the *House of Magic & Mysticism*. The two of you are soulmates who can create magic together. You are happy simply being each other's confidante. The Dragon and Snake have a powerful cosmic relationship and make excellent partners building a life together. You communicate at many levels and there is wonderful humour in this pairing.

When Dragon and Snake come together, you never quarrel over the details or who gets to do what, because

HOUSES OF PAIRED SOULMATES

ANIMALS	YIN/ YANG	ZODIAC HOUSE	TARGET UNLEASHED
Rat & Ox	YANG /YIN	*House of Creativity & Cleverness*	The Rat initiates The Ox completes
Tiger & Rabbit	YANG /YIN	*House of Growth & Development*	The Tiger uses strength The Rabbit uses negotiation
Dragon & Snake	YANG /YIN	*House of Magic & Spirituality*	The Dragon takes action The Snake creates magic
Horse & Sheep	YANG /YIN	*House of Passion & Sexuality*	The Horse embodies strength & courage The Sheep embodies seduction & allure
Monkey & Rooster	YANG /YIN	*House of Career & Commerce*	The Monkey creates good strategy The Rooster takes timely action
Dog & Boar	YANG /YIN	*House of Domesticity*	The Dog creates alliances The Boar benefits

you understand each other's unique strengths and assets. You bring out the best in each other, and are as happy whether your relationship is a personal or professional one.

3. Secret Friends

Another extremely powerful affinity arises when two secret friends come together. There are six pairs of secret friends in the Zodiac. Love, respect and goodwill flow freely between you. Once forged, your bond is extremely hard to break. Even when you yourselves want to break it, it will be hard for either party to walk away. This pair of signs will stick together through thick and thin. For the Dragon, your secret friend is the Rooster. This is a very synergistic coupling as there is a mutual adoration and easy comradeship that springs forth spontaneously when you are together. The Dragon is excellent for the Rooster and vice versa.

PAIRINGS OF SECRET FRIENDS			
🐀	Rat	Ox	🐂
🐖	Boar	Tiger	🐅
🐕	Dog	Rabbit	🐇
🐉	Dragon	Rooster	🐓
🐍	Snake	Monkey	🐒
🐎	Horse	Sheep	🐑

These are two signs who are not only passionate as lovers, they are best friends as well. When the Dragon gets together with someone of the Rooster sign, there is real chance of long term happiness, and even when difficulties crop up, there is every chance you will both emerge out of it even stronger. The Dragon and Rooster enjoy a very special bond which prevails whatever the circumstances.

4. Peach Blossom Links

Each alliance of allies has a special relationship with one of the four primary signs of Horse, Rat, Rooster and Rabbit in that these are the symbolic representations of love and romance for one alliance group of animal signs. These are referred to as Peach Blossom Animals, and the presence of their images in the homes of the matching alliance of allies brings peach blossom luck, which is associated with love and romance.

The Dragon belongs to the alliance of Dragon, Monkey and Rat, which has the Rooster as their Peach Blossom link.

There is underlying passion between the Dragon and Rooster. Because the Rooster is your Peach Blossom link, displaying Roosters in the home brings love and marriage luck to the Dragon.

The Dragon benefits from associating with anyone born in the Rooster year, and will also benefit from placing a painting or image of a Rooster in the West part of the house, or in the Dragon direction of SE. The Rooster is also the secret friend of the Dragon, making this connection doubly auspicious.

5. Seasonal Trinities

Another grouping of signs creates the *seasonal trinity* combinations that bring the luck of *seasonal abundance*. To many experts, this is regarded one of the more powerful combinations. When it exists within a family made up of either parent or both parents with one or more children, it indicates that as a family unit, their collective luck can transform all that is negative into positive indications. When annual indications of the year are not favourable, the existence of a seasonal combination of signs in any living abode can transform bad luck into better luck, especially during the season indicated by the combination.

Seasonal Trinities of the Horoscope

ANIMAL SIGNS	SEASON	ELEMEMT	DIRECTION
Dragon, Rabbit, Tiger	*Spring*	Wood	East
Snake, Horse, Sheep	*Summer*	Fire	South
Monkey, Rooster, Dog	*Autumn*	Metal	West
Ox, Rat, Boar	*Winter*	Water	North

It is necessary for all three signs to live together or be in the same office working in close proximity for this powerful pattern to work. For greater impact, it is better if they are all using the direction associated with the relevant season. The Dragon belongs to the Spring Season, its direction is East, and its seasonal group comprises the Tiger, Rabbit and Dragon.

6. Astrological Enemies

Your astrological enemy is the sign that directly confronts yours in the astrology wheel. For the Dragon, your astrological enemy is the Dog. Note that your enemy does not necessarily harm you; it only means someone of this sign can never be of any real help to you. There is a six year gap between natural enemies. A marriage between astroligical enemies is not usually

PAIRINGS OF ASTROLOGICAL ENEMIES		
Rat	⟷	Horse
Boar	⟷	Snake
Dog	⟷	Dragon
Rabbit	⟷	Rooster
Tiger	⟷	Monkey
Ox	⟷	Sheep

recommended. Thus marriage between a Dragon and Dog is unlikely to bring lasting happiness unless other indications suggest otherwise. The Dragon is advised to refrain from getting involved with anyone born in the year of the Dog, although on a year-by-year basis, this can sometimes be overcome by the annual energies. As a business partnership, this pairing is likely to lead to problems, and in the event of a split, the separation is often acrimonious and painful. Even if passion flows between you at the early stages of your relationship, you are not likely to be happy together in the long run.

The Dragon and Dog are better off not marrying or living together as partners. Even when there is love flowing back and forth during the initial stages, you are unlikely to be close over the long term. Note however that astrological opposites can coexist quite harmoniously as friends or siblings.

If a Dragon is already married to a Dog, the solution to improve your prospects for lasting happiness is to introduce the secret friend of each other into your living space. This can be done through the symbolic use of figurines or art. As a pair, you should thus display the secret friend of the Dragon, the **Rooster**, and the secret friend of the Dog, the **Rabbit**, in the home.

DRAGON with RAT
Supporting each other
through a challenging year

Dragon and Rat always make a fabulous pair! They are allies of the Zodiac and when they come together, they produce a comradeship that is very hard to beat.

In 2021, both are going through a challenging year, so neither has the upper hand when it comes to its luck profile, but Dragon & Rat are always stronger together than apart. Rat feels safe and secure with the Dragon, while Dragon is energised by the perky optimism of the Rat.

Dragon and Rat always build each other up. When faced with a common enemy or dilemma, they close ranks and are stronger together. They boost each other's confidence and bring out the very best in one another. Rat feels secure in Dragon's warm embrace, and Dragon is empowered by Rat's flattery and charm. Both have big egos, but each will happily boost the other's self-assurance, so they make a very beneficial couple indeed. Dragon and Rat are happy whether working alongside striving for a common goal, or propping the other up while each works towards its own individual aspirations. Whether romantic or platonic, this pairing always makes for a formidable team.

In 2021, Rat suffers low energy, while Dragon has the Five Yellow; both are strong Earth afflictions that need dealing with. **Metal element energy** will help both signs, but so will each other's invaluable support. When Rat and Dragon get together, they think more of each other than themselves. Both are naturally self-centered personalities, but when together, they take adopt far more nurturing and selfless personas.

If Rat falls for a Dragon in 2021, even if both face external challenges, their natural affinity will carry them along. Whatever they choose to put their attention on, when they have the backing of the other, they are sure to attain their goals. For this pair, the journey is more important than the destination, and there will be plenty of laughs along the way. They are natural comedians and will always look at the glass half-full. As a couple, they are the ultimate optimists.

It is difficult for Dragon to find a more compatible partner than the Rat, and vice versa, so if you have just found each other, take joy and do everything in your power to make things work. You have an extremely bright future together!

DRAGON with OX
Difficult with two captains

Dragon and Ox are not immediately compatible, but they can form a firm friendship as long as they do not get too close. As friends or colleagues, they work well together. They are both ambitious and motivated, and each has the stamina and endurance to stay the course even in the most challenging of situations. When they join forces to face a dilemma, their resolute natures make them a brilliant team.

Dragon and Ox have very different personalities. They hold different things dear to them, and so building a life together may prove tricky.

This stems mainly from the fact that both are strong personalities. Ox is pragmatic and sensible, while Dragon is impetuous and a dreamer. When together too long, each will want to take charge of setting the course for the future, and in a relationship, it will be difficult to have two captains.

These two signs work best when they come together on a project-by-project basis. When their goals are clearly defined and the endgame is mutually agreed upon from the start, they accept each other's ideas with enthusiasm and acceptance. In fact, the greater the task at hand, or the bigger the crisis, the better these two will get along, because then they understand that two heads are better than one. When things slip back to normality, each will find it difficult to take a back seat. These are both natural leaders who want to take command, and eventually, their clashing personalities will become a problem between them.

> In love, Dragon and Ox can have a passionate love affair, with Dragon leading the dance in the arms of a strong and steady Ox. But dance too long and the Ox will tire of Dragon's fanciful moves, while Dragon will break free from what it considers Ox's monotonous steps.

There can be short term chemistry between these two, but venture into marriage, and they will have to try put in colossal effort to keep the passion alive.

Dragon and Ox get on best when they are platonic and having something to sink their teeth in together. When working on the same team, their talents can work in tandem and they can produce brilliant results together. In 2021, Ox has the edge over the Dragon, so it helps both if Ox takes the lead. But the Dragon may not stay too happy about this arrangement for long.

DRAGON with TIGER

Different approaches lead to much dissent

Dragon and Tiger are never a good match and the energies of 2021 only exacerbate their differences. The thing is, Dragon and Tiger are too alike in their need for power and to be in charge for a tenable partnership to ever arise between them. Indeed, even as friends, there will be frequent quarrels and blow-ups, making it impossible for either side to properly trust the other.

Both these signs pride themselves as morally upright and principled. They would never betray a friend, and they stand by their comrades through thick and thin. But the animosity that easily arises between Dragon and Tiger can cause both these signs to go against their very nature.

If one betrays the other in even the smallest of ways, the other will be hell-bent on revenge, and will not stop until it achieves it.

In 2021, the Dragon is terribly afflicted by the *Five Yellow* in its sector, together with the *Yearly Killings Star* from the 24 Mountains. The Tiger enjoys better luck overall, but its magnification star amplifies all that is unfavourable with Dragon, bringing disaster to the relationship. Unfortunately, with these two, even though both may be extremely gifted, beautifully creative and powerfully resilient, when together they break down each other's defenses one by one, till nothing is left bu what is negative and undesirable. They are no good for one another's confidence, and try as they may to be friends, it is a difficult pairing to get right.

No astrologer would ever advise this as a favourable match, and in 2021, everything becomes much more hazardous still.

FENG SHUI CURE: If already together, a Dragon and Tiger pairing will need to display the secret friends of each other in the living space they share. This will help to smooth things over between them. They need the **Rooster** and the **Boar**.

As colleagues or work mates, the advice is not to get too close. Keep an arm's length and stay completely professional in your interactions with each other. Dragon and Tiger's talents can combine to create wonderful things, but when your personalities are involved, it ruins everything you try to do together.

DRAGON with RABBIT

Passion and romance await these two!

Dragon and Rabbit have similar tastes and an ability to work well together and although they sometimes see an occasional disagreement, generally this is a peaceful match which brings happiness and love to both. The Dragon is a dominating kind of person and the Rabbit accepts this, and is in fact attracted to it, hence there is little difficulty here. These two will have few problems building a nest together as they tend to have a natural preference for the same things. They both belong to the season of Spring, bringing strong growth energy to the relationship should they come together as a couple.

> In 2021, when Rabbit has the Peach Blossom Star in its sector, this union is blessed not just with shared ideals and ambitions, but passion and romance as well.

Neither Dragon nor Rabbit are the seriously competitive type when it comes to their loved ones. This is a relationship that does not get spoilt by petty or complicated egos clashing. The Dragon has no problem creating a stable relationship with the Rabbit, as they are both able to see the big picture and instinctively work towards achieving results they both desire. This characteristic makes an excellent basis to create something potentially sound and lasting together.

When it comes to forging a united front to deal with troublemakers from the outside trying to upset their equilibrium, this pair is also very on the ball. Their loyalty to one another is stable, and is the secret of their resilience and also their happiness. The Dragon can fly as high or as far as it wishes, and the Rabbit is always nearby offering support and a helping hand.

This year, Rabbit enjoys infinitely better luck indications than Dragon, so it gives its powerful friend a leg up. But Rabbit gets inspired by Dragon's untiring vigour and lust for life, because even when hit by the troublesome *Five Yellow*, the passionate Dragon does not let its light get dimmed.

A relationship between Dragon and Rabbit is extremely auspicious for both. The energies of 2021 may see Rabbit playing a more prominent part in the relationship, and their regular roles may get reversed for the time being, with Dragon supporting Rabbit from the sidelines. But the good thing with this union is that neither have a problem with playing second fiddle to the other. If Dragon and Rabbit come together, the truest of love can grow.

DRAGON with DRAGON

Plenty of laughs but no true loyalty

Two Dragons will either be great friends or bitter enemies. They possess strong characters and unless there are strong bonds putting them naturally on the same side, it is unlikely that this can be much of a partnership. Should they be romantically attached, it is likely they have carved out their respective spheres within the relationship so one does not step on the toes of the other.

While two Dragons can find happiness together, they will also develop as two independents rather than merge as one entity.

In 2021, the Dragon is afflicted from various corners, with the Five Yellow being their biggest stumbling block. A Dragon in the arms of another Dragon will find little comfort and consolation. Each will be too busy nursing its own grievances to provide much reassurance to the other.

If two Dragons meet this year, they are unlikely to fall head over heels, simply because neither will have the energy to do much pursuing. Neither will make any serious moves and the relationship is then unlikely to take off. For the Dragon to fall in love this year, it needs a more aggressive suitor. The Dragon needs to be swept off its feet, similar to what it would do if it were the one doing the pursuing. And alas, another Dragon will be just as lukewarm about love and romance.

> Two Dragons will get along better in a work or platonic relationship in 2021 than a romantic one, as there will be less expectation, and Dragons are generally responsible and dependable characters, unlikely to let emotions or personal issues get in the way of work well done. And two Dragons will certainly get the work done.

As friends, two Dragons share plenty of laughs and be great relief for each other in a year fraught with obstacles and mishaps. But neither Dragon can expect another Dragon mate to be a true confidante in times of real need. For that kind of friendship, a Dragon will have to look elsewhere.

If two Dragons get pitted against one another, they are the competitive kind and are likely to fight to the death. When they are after the same goal, promotion or love interest, any loyalty for friendship's sake goes out the window. While two Dragons can work, it will always be fraught with difficulties. Not the most ideal of matches if they get too close.

DRAGON with SNAKE

Making a fabulous team in 2021

Dragon and Snake always make a magical and enviable pair. They are soulmates of the Chinese Zodiac, forming the *House of Magic and Mysticism* together. If committed to one another, their loyalty is steadfast and true. They genuinely enjoy each other's company and there is also great respect. Dragon is smitten by the seductive Snake, and Snake is bowled over by the charismatic Dragon.

For Dragon and Snake, they are always in their honeymoon period. These two do not take themselves too seriously when with each other. They laugh and joke, even at each other's expense, without batting an eyelash.

They communicate almost telepathically and they have the same interests and ideals. Even if their hobbies and life goals are different, they quickly get behind each other's dreams and have a meaningful hand at helping make them come true. Between them pulsates a cosmic love that stands the test of time. If married, they may drift apart now and then, but they always come back together. They are rarely unfaithful, so there is little danger from temptation by third parties. Both hold their own in the relationship, and they are truly a pairing of equals in every sense. Rarely will you see a Dragon and Snake where one is the breadwinner and the other the homemaker. No, they share out all their mutual tasks so their lives never get boring.

Both Dragon and Snake are multi-talented, able to juggle many different balls at once, and slip into various family tasks and responsibilities seamlessly. You are just as likely to see the father parent in a Dragon-Snake coupling at a parent conference as you are the mother; and neither is likely to be financially dependent on the other.

> As workmates, Dragon and Snake are a dream team. They rarely quarrel, and they divide up tasks with no hassle at all. They rarely have to "check" with each other before making a decision, and they never play the blame game.

In 2021, both suffer from the *Five Yellow* affliction in their shared home sector, but they weather this storm together. Their numbers join to form the auspicious sum-of-ten. There is great empathy between them, and, they are likely to transform misfortune into good fortune simply from the positivity they stir up in each other. A match made in heaven indeed!

DRAGON with HORSE
This unlikely match blessed by the heavens in 2021

Dragon and Horse may not make your most likely match, but all this changes in 2021. The year brings some magical energies the way of the Horse, who becomes especially alluring to the mighty Dragon. This year Horse is a real winner, with the victory star on its side, and also the blessings of the *Golden Deity*. If a Horse catches the eye of a Dragon, the Dragon can hardly resist.

In 2021, Dragon & Horse can look forward to wonderful adventures together, with Horse leading the charge. In love, there is unbridled passion, and in work, both keep the other motivated and driven.

So much good energy flows between a Dragon and a Horse this year. In this relationship, it is often the Dragon who plays leader, driving the relationship from its viewpoint and agenda, but in 2021, Dragon is happy to let Horse take the reins for a while. These two signs are equally impetuous, courageous and impulsive, but instead of this being a recipe for disaster, they bring each other excitement and success. They form strong bonds in 2021, and if in a love relationship, they will make the sheets burn with passion.

This is not a year when their energies are well-matched. Dragon is stronger from an element luck perspective, while Horse is stronger with good flying stars. Horse has the added benefit of not one but two *Big Auspicious* stars. But together with a Dragon, the Horse finds the courage and discipline to transform opportunities into success.

Theirs is a big picture environment and their worlds are coloured by long strokes of the paintbrush. Both relish challenges and have independent spirits that refuse to be restrained. Thus conventions and traditions never get in their way. They are strongly supportive and loyal with never a dull moment.

Infidelities, if any, are swept into oblivion by the tide of their own passion for each other. Neither are the petty kind, so they can make blunder after blunder and still forgive and forget. For them, they understand that choices are not made in a void; and if in the process of a decision one hurts or slights the other, they will not hold a grudge as long as the hurt was unintentional. This gives the relationship incredible resilience, especially in an afflicted year when blunders will be made. A charming coupling where the pleasures outweigh any pain.

DRAGON with SHEEP

Uncomfortable relationship
where both are quarrelsome

Dragon and Sheep are two Earth signs that can work in a conducive year, but 2021 is not such a year. These two individuals make for a vibrant relationship when one clearly dominates. They are also better when they are each pursuing their own thing. When they lead separate lives as well as the one they share with one another, then their union can blossom into a long-lasting partnership.

In truth, they do not have all that much in common. It is easy to list their differences as they tend to be many and wide-ranging. Their styles differ, as do their aspirations and values. They look at life and the world through different lenses. And so, often, when they attempt to walk the same road, it is like walking a road to nowhere. Sooner or later, they realise this and could well be tempted to part ways.

They are not helped in 2021 as Sheep is troubled by the quarrelsome star, making it more irritable than usual. Dragon does nothing to soothe its tempers, so things may get noisy and heated in a Sheep and Dragon pairing this year.

When both go through good years, these two can make for a beautiful union, as Sheep is in awe of Dragon's magnetism, while Dragon gets roped in by Sheep's seductive ways. There will be no tussle for control, as Sheep happily yields to Dragon's natural dominance. But in years like this one, both may tend to act out of character as they are hardly helped by the energies afflicting them. Dragon is more fiery than usual, and so is the Sheep. Gone then is the dreamy elegance that they can share in the early stages of a courtship.

If Dragon and Sheep meet this year, it is unlikely that any real attraction will take root. They simply cannot recognise all that is positive in each other.

In a work relationship, things are better between Dragon and Sheep, especially when they do not get too close or too comfortable with one another. They are different enough to bring varied skills and talents to the mix, and the result could bring much success and productivity. But because of the quarrelsome energies in the air, it is better if one is the clear boss and the other the subordinate. When you put a Dragon and Sheep together on equal footing, the year may see them butt heads more frequently than marching in tandem.

DRAGON with MONKEY

Sympatico through good times & bad

It is difficult to find a better pairing than a Dragon and Monkey. These two are so in sync that they can converse without actually talking! They breathe and think the same way, yet are different enough that they combine such that the whole becomes far more than their parts.

In 2021, things may well be noisier for this pair than usual, as Monkey is afflicted by the quarrelsome star and Dragon has the Five Yellow, but their intrinsic affinity overcomes any minor obstacles they may encounter.

Yes they may argue and quarrel, but they always make up so quickly you would never guess they ever held any differences. Neither are the type to hold a grudge, so they rarely trip up so badly to make things irreconciliable. And they never air their dirty laundry in public. To the rest of the world, these two when paired up always project the most united of fronts.

The wonderful thing about this pairing is the incredible energy they have when together. They are both part of the competitive trinity of the Zodiac, and they love nothing better than hatching grand plans to make money and to conquer the world. They are both

ambitious and shrewd to a degree that would frighten anyone who happens to find themselves pitted against them.

> While romance will not be the mainstay of the relationship, there is plenty of passion between these two. They know how to enjoy life, and together, they fuel each other's great lust for living.

They enjoy great adventures together and will never let something like money stop them. Not for this pair overbudgeting. They will tend to spend first and worry later. They live life on the edge and are willing to take big risks. Whether in love or in work, they move with big bold strides without blinking an eye or batting an eyelash. Their confidence is phenomenal and magnified when together.

At work and in business, a Dragon and Monkey pair make a dream team! Their collaboration at the workplace is unrivalled, making them quite unbeatable together. They are both high flyers who keep their mind on the job, and when motivated, become deadly focused. They give each other a big boost, so this pairing will always be more remarkable together than singly. Really, you cannot find a better pair.

DRAGON with ROOSTER

Rooster gives Dragon a leg up in 2021

The Dragon and Rooster pairing are one of the ultimate in the Chinese Zodiac. When they come together, they represent the celestial Dragon and Phoenix, the king of the land matched with the king of the birds, the symbol of the Emperor. These are two signs that work well under any circumstance. Whether they are a married couple, business partners, best friends or colleagues, their chemistry together is undeniable.

These two signs personify the synergy of two complementary but opposite sides of a coin. As a couple, both are clever enough to appreciate the advantages of the union, so it is easy to exchange thoughts and ideas in a constructive way. A healthy respect for each other enables love to flow freely and seamlessly.

> Dragon and Rooster are secret friends of the Zodiac, making them beneficial for each other whether they intend to be or not, and no matter how hard or how little they try.

In 2021, Rooster enjoys far stronger luck than Dragon in every respect, with superior element luck and the prosperity star. Dragon has the *Five Yellow* and other afflictions, but with a Rooster mate by its side, Dragon gets the boost it needs to make the year a very happy and successful one.

They are always supportive of each other. And because both are strong cosmic signs, there is a celestial elegance in the way they love and live together. They have what other combinations do not. They make a very exciting match that manifests a special potential, that of transforming misfortune into good fortune opportunities.

They become perfect antidotes for each other's afflictions, and this is exactly the case for the Dragon this year. A Dragon with a Rooster finds it the key to solving all its problems, trials and tribulations whenever they crop up in 2021.

They inspire each other in very special ways, taking risks in their relationship that others would not. In this sense, there are bound to be clashes now and then, and because both are fiery signs, their conflicts can be startling to onlookers. But while both love and feel deeply, they are among the most level-headed of the Zodiac and will not let emotions ruin what is important. They may adore the drama of a spectacle, but they are excellent performers, so their outbursts are often merely for show. A stable pair always full of fire and excitement.

DRAGON with DOG

Deep incompatibility worsens in 2021

Dragon and Dog are not good for one another. They bring out the worst in each other, constantly finding fault and generally causing all kinds of negative instincts to surface. They do not make a good couple either living or working together. If they do come together because of initial attraction, the superficiality of their relationship quickly becomes evident. It will be difficult for Dragon and Dog to last beyond a few first dates.

The only way this union will work well if is at least one has the ascendant of the other in its birth chart. If one of them is born in the hour of the other e.g. if the Dog is born in the hour of the Dragon (7am to 9am), or Dragon is born in the hour of the Dog (7pm to 9pm).

The other way to fix a bad union that has already happened is to form the Earth Cross within the family. If a pair of Dragon and Dog parents have children born in the Ox and Sheep here, the four signs together create good fortune. But this does not mean Dragon and Dog will get along; it simply means their joint success together smooths things over in their personal relationship.

True compatibility between a Dragon and Dog is difficult to achieve, and this is even more of a case in 2021, when neither are going through an easy year.

In 2021, the Dragon suffers from the Five Yellow affliction, so will have its fair share or troubles to deal with. Dog meanwhile has the Loss Star in its sector. Both will be too busy fixing their own problems to give much time or comfort to the other.

With the Dog, Dragon's courage and valour becomes foolhardiness; and with the Dragon, Dog's loyalty becomes neediness. Neither brings out what is positive in the other, and instead, transforms strengths into negatives. Not a good match.

Dog is disdainful of Dragon's ideas and opinions; and Dragon finds the Dog unsupportive and a wet blanket. The match is an example of clashing personalities. Not only is there little communication, there is much exhaling in exasperation on the part of the Dragon, and a great deal of barking from the Dog! Better to look elsewhere if you are looking for long-term happiness.

DRAGON with BOAR

Neither great nor terrible together

While this match may not be the most exciting or dynamic of duos in the Zodiac, it has a good chance of developing into something comfortable that can last. Their temperaments balance each other out, with Boar's congeniality harmonizing well with Dragon's flamboyance. Dragon will provide the excitement and adventure in this relationship, while Boar keeps them grounded.

Both are social animals, so they make a wonderfully popular couple in whatever circles they move in. This is a good thing because a Dragon and Boar will need more than just each other to sustain themselves. They play off each other well, but are rather better in company than when alone. When left with just each other for company for too long, the cracks will begin to appear, and their general kindness towards each other may wear off.

In 2021, this relationship is unlikely to work well, as both have to endure various afflictions through the year. Neither will be the strong arms the other needs to be embraced in during times of tribulation.

This coupling works better when everything is peachy. They do not face crises well together, and in times of calamity, one or both could be tempted into the arms of another offering comfort or sympathy. They are not immune to being unfaithful, and when one strays, the other will find it hard to forgive.

If ever there is a case of infidelity, even if these two stay together, the lone incident will be enough to drive a wedge that eventually rips them apart. And 2021 poses just this kind of risk.

In work and business, Dragon and Boar combine well as both are easy-going personalities with a good sense of humour. They laugh their way out of tight spots and never take themselves too seriously. But neither will be a particular source of motivation for the other.

In general, Dragon and Boar will get along, if only in lukewarm fashion. They are neither great for each other nor terrible. If their goals align, they can make a good team working towards such shared goals, but theirs will never be the kind of relationship to ignite much fire or passion. If either are looking for that in a relationship, they will have to look elsewhere.

Dragon's Monthly Horoscope 2021

Chapter 6

Big dreams and potential, but needs better staying power

The Dragon has fabulous success luck indications this year, so the potential is definitely there for big achievements and accolades. But because your sign has low spirit essence and various afflictions, you could find yourself wanting to give up at the slightest difficulty. You need to fight the urge to give in to weariness when things don't go your way. Don't let the opinions of others matter so much. There is much to look forward to if you can stop making excuses or getting distracted when the going gets tough. When you start something, see it through. If you can finish what you start, the end results can be astonishing.

1st Month
February 4th - March 5th 2021

STARTING THE YEAR WELL WITH FRIENDS

The Dragon starts the year off on the right foot. You have an army of allies by your side and no end of people willing to help if you only speak up and ask. In fact, relationship luck is so overwhelmingly powerful that even your "rivals" and those who envied you previously see your good points and are happy to be your friend! You discover common interests in people you never identified as friends before, and your social network expands rapidly, especially if you work at it. The good news is that with all this attention you are getting, you can match each for enthusiasm, so it is easy to make new friends. Your gregarious self wins out, making this is very happy month for you!

Work & Career - *Making an impression*

You are filled with many ideas concerning work and implementing them to your company's benefit seems easy. Those higher-up who may not have even acknowledged you in the past sit up and take notice. New opportunities to shine open up, so make the most of them. Your bosses and those higher up the food chain are willing to listen to your ideas, and you have a good number of good ones. The Dragon is a natural people person, so when you put your heart and mind to it, winning others over comes quite naturally. How well you do and how many rungs up the career ladder you can leapfrog only depends on how much work you are willing to put in. Your level of success is thus up to you.

Your luck holds strong putting others firmly on your side and shielding you from would-be rivals. A time to take big strides and cover good ground.

Business - *The Pied Piper*

Making contacts comes easily to you, as people find you charming and genuine. The Dragon is the ultimate showman. When you want to impress, you are a smooth talker and you inject your conversation with just the right amount of wit and wisdom. As the life of any party or discussion, it is easy for you to win others over. A good month for cutting new deals, tying up with strategic partners and making the big changes.

Your strength now is in networking, so make the most of this. Getting to know people is easy enough, but your talent is making them come onto your side. Not all introductions routinely lead to friendship, but you are an exception as even strangers take a liking to you upon first meeting. As a boss or leader, you are effective at motivating those who work for you, so keep putting in effort here.

ENHANCER: Wear the **mystic knot symbol strung with onyx** to boost your triple luck of networking, business success and career growth. Don't let your popularity go to waste this month - wear the **Precious Horse and Popularity Talisman** to make the most of your great charm or carry the **"Ah" Dakini Popularity Amulet**.

Love & Relationships - *Passionate & popular*

There are plenty of romantic encounters on the cards and passion runs high. Better play safe and go out with those who are available. If you consort with married individuals, you may be caught out and the results will not be pretty. Your social life is hectic, but you thrive on being appreciated for your sparkling presence. Single Dragons are in for a marvelous time!

Education - *Feeling motivated*

Your powers of concentration are all pervasive and you are attracted to many things. Previous topics you barely had time to think about now seem fascinating. You realize school life is more than good grades. More importantly, you are self-motivated and need little impetus to get you to open your books. Learning becomes pure joy and the more you achieve, the more driven you become.

2nd Month
March 6th - April 4th 2021

....

QUARRELSOME CHI
MAKES YOU DISAGREEABLE

The energies of the month cause the Dragon to be hot tempered and quick to criticize. This makes you much harder to get along with, and even you should admit it is mostly your own doing if things don't work out and people shy away. Even if you are in the right, excessive pointing of other people's failings will not endear you to anyone. Even those by the sidelines are wary lest you pick on them. To play it safe, keep a low profile, avoid self-publicity and steer clear from grey areas.

You can be held liable by law if things go wrong, so check with company lawyers before you sign on the dotted line. More so if it involves personal affairs like loans or borrowings.

....

Work & Career - *Argumentative*

If you find the workplace a drag, it is probably your own fault. You are argumentative and demanding, making you are a pain to work with, which explains why colleagues are so reluctant to cooperate! Be prepared to admit your mistakes when you are patently wrong. A simple apology works wonders and restores the equilibrium which is sorely lacking in your life now.

Forget about impressing the boss; any attempt will probably backfire and make you appear scheming and manipulative.

Too much interaction is not a good idea since the energies of the month are against you. Socializing should be minimized as you already face stiff competition, so concentrate on the work on hand instead of being too ambitious.

Business - *Legal problems*

Keep frustrations to yourself as the less people know your feelings, the better. This is not the best time to venture into new partnerships or projects. Instead, focus on positive human relations and support existing staff that show promise. Encourage or even sponsor them to take specific courses that have a direct bearing on your company. Promoting them to new levels will reap benefits, since you will need their newfound skills later to increase sales.

Contain your annoyances as making a fuss will only make things worse. There are delays and obstacles which seem unavoidable, so live with it. This phase occurs to everyone and now just happens to be your turn. Avoid getting into trouble with the law as there is real possibility of legal problems.

Love & Relationships - *Difficult*

If you are looking for peace and harmony in your love life, avoid a triangular affair! Whether married or involved, a third party may enter to severely upset the equilibrium. Since you are the one holding the key, the ball is in your court whether to nip it in the bud or allow the illicit affair to bloom.

Married Dragons get easily exasperated with their spouses but this is no excuse to look elsewhere for succour. Be more tolerant of minor failings, since you are far from perfection personified yourself. Singles can wait for another time to hook up. Diving into a new relationship now will only lead to an equally rushed break-up sooner rather than later. If looking to enter a relationship that lasts, the advice is to take things slow.

Education - *Emotionally rattled*

Friendships go through a rocky patch, and the month may see your social circles changing and evolving. New people enter your life which may not please you initially. Your mind is rattled, and you can't seem to concentrate because of relationship troubles. Don't let them get to you. You can't expect to popular all the time.

CURE FOR THE MONTH: Carry the **Apple Peace Amulet** to alleviate the irritable energies this month; it will also help you smooth over troubled relationships.

3rd Month
April 5th - May 5th 2021

FEELING LISTLESS AND LACKING IN ENERGY

You would think you are in line for some respite after the frustrations of last month but no, you must hang on a little longer. This month is hardly better as now you have health worries. You are particularly susceptible to viruses doing the rounds, so take extra care. Falling sick now is not just miserable, it could have serious knock-on effects vis a vis your work and career. Look after yourself and don't take your health for granted. Don't drive carelessly and no rough sports this month, since your defences are down and you are liable to injure yourself for no good reason. If you can, avoid long distance travel as moving from place to place attracts bad chi energies for you.

Work & Career - *Firm up friendships*

Your career is not going great guns. You need to develop closer relationships with those you work with daily. Success comes from having support, and allies who believe in you have never been more important, so get going building those bonds. You may have no choice but to call on a few favours, but there is nothing embarrassing asking for help, so go for it. Some may be only too willing to return the favour since you may have helped them previously. Set reasonable targets you know are achievable; don't burn yourself out slaving away.

Success comes from getting along with colleagues whose level of co-operation will impact directly on your work quality.

Business - *Lie low*

Wealth luck is down and so is your morale. Even your staff are affected, but it is up to you to keep up motivation and be cheerleader. Not easy when you are feeling rather pessimistic and under the weather yourself. Closing deals is beset with problems, minor or major. You have to work doubly hard just to maintain the momentum you have built up. Things don't come easy and sales figures could be lackluster. You are eager to launch new projects to replenish your diminishing coffers, but be careful these new ventures don't turn into white elephants!

For now it is best to avoid radical pursuits, however promising they seem. Once involved, hidden costs may start appearing. Cash should be conserved, not spent. Avoid new investments and large expeditures, as the more money flows out, the worse it gets for business, as returns are unpredictable. Lie low, avoid taking risks, book yourself a vacation if you must.

Love & Relationships - *Support*

The bright spot this month is your personal life, which seems glittering compared to what you face at work! Those attached will find your partner a great source of support, or a shoulder to cry on, whichever it is you need. Single Dragons may enter too quickly into a new relationhip simply to feel you have someone in your corner. But if you rush into something without being sure, don't be surprised if things don't last very long. On the other hand, who knows? You may well stumble upon your soulmate, with this desperation forcing you to be less choosy. Could turn out a blessing in disguise.

Education - *Forming friendships*

You are not in top form, so avoid dangerous sports since you are prone to injuries. Working in study groups helps you because you are not feeling up to facing everything on your own. Forming mutually beneficial alliances will help when it comes to studies, and could even make you some lasting friendships.

> **CURE FOR THE MONTH:** The Dragon really needs to carry health amulets this month. Don't take your health for granted. You should also keep health enhancers in the SE and sleep with your head pointed to your *Tien Yi* direction. Carry the **Medicine Buddha Amulet.**

4th Month
May 6th - June 5th 2021

VICTORY STAR BRINGS NEW HOPE

Your luck takes a turn for the better and good luck arrives by the containerload! Some big changes are also heading your way. They are all for the better so there is no need to worry. This is a month of new beginnings, of turning over a new leaf, acquiring new skills and making the changes in your life that may be long overdue. No need to hesitate - if something has not been working for a while, make the neccessary changes. Stalling will only waste valuable time, and if ever your luck can withstand big shifts, it is now. The future becomes clear and you know what must be done. Follow your instincts which will not let you down this month. Besides, you have the *Victory Star* on your side, so coming out on top naturally follows.

Work & Career - *Impressing the boss*

You can be hugely successful this month! All you need do is perform as usual. Your efforts at this time get noticed and appreciated. You can impress the boss with all of your leadership prowess coming to the fore. You may even be asked handle more people or subordinates, giving you another chance to prove your skills. You are confident and assured of your talents, so think positive. You may be transferred to another department, get a pay raise, get promoted or receive a new portfolio. You may get some new additions to the team, some of whom become valuable allies. Whatever is thrown at you, take it in your stride.

ENHANCER FOR THE MONTH:
Display the **Desktop Victory Flag** in the SE and carry the **Windhorse Success Amulet**. You benefit from winning luck this month, and the best way for making this ripen for you is to activate with effective enhancers.

Business - *Expansion*

Be bold in investing, expanding and launching new initiatives. Your luck holds strong and plans set in motion now bring rich rewards later. This is the time to consider moving in new directions. Diversification leads to greater creativity and will help cross-fertilize with your current business strategies, improving your existing workflows. Don't be averse to getting involved in too many things. The more active you stay, the better all round. Others look up to you for leadership, so make an effort to provide it. You have the power to motivate and inspire this month, so make an effort to do so. Solidify personal relationships with your staff without necessarily becoming too familiar. But showing empathy and having occasional social occasions together will only strengthen their loyalty.

Love & Relationships - *Wonderful*

A good month for love and romance. You are not short of suitors and admirers. There is great happiness in store in the near future; this can mean a fabulous night, relationship or engagement. Whatever the case, it is an occasion to celebrate. If looking to get married, this is an ideal time to propose or make plans. If you are already engaged, now is also a suitable time to get married. For the long married couple, if you notice your hobbies and interests beginning to diverge, do something about it. Make an effort to be more involved in your partner's schemes or you may slowly drift apart. You perform better in the driver's seat.

Home & Family - *Satisfying*

Your family makes you proud this month as one or more achieve something notable that pleases you. There may be new family members joining the clan due to marriage or birth.

Education - *Coming out tops*

Anything new you sink your teeth in now will take off, whether assignments, projects, fundraising or social activities. The more competitive you allow yourself to be, the more obvious your success. Enjoy the month as there are many joyful moments in store.

5th Month
June 6th - July 6th 2021

MISFORTUNE LUCK GETS MAGNIFIED. BEWARE.

The resident *Five Yellow* gets a boost with the magnification star paying a visit, putting a big dampener on your luck. The #9 star boosts your energy levels but also throws up difficult situations you will not be expecting. Things do not run smooth and obstacles crop up in a variety of guises. Remain alert so that surprises do not catch you out. Remember there are solutions to everything. You just need to spend time looking for them. Things work themselves out eventually, but in the meantime don't lose hope. Keep your cool or you risk ruining a few relationships. Accept help when it is offered to you.

Work & Career - *Reading the nuances*

There are many small ups and downs, so be prepared to adjust the way you work. Reading the nuances in any situation becomes more important because small actions draw big reactions. Take advantage of your sprightlier energy to impress superiors and colleagues. Working smart trumps slaving away this month. When you strike the right chord, whatever you do is well received. And vice versa. So put more attention on appearances and how you are coming across. There may well be some fierce competition at the office. Because there is a lot at stake, you need to make sure you come out victorious. Don't take for granted that politics in the office will blow over if you stay above the fray. If you become somebody's target, things can turn unpleasant very quickly. This is a time when it is better to fight when challenged than to simply give in and hope to remain everybody's friend.

A month when reading the nuances is important because small actions draw big reactions.

Business - *Trust your instincts*

Your ego may have taken a bruising, causing you to lose confidence. This leads you to seek the opinions of others more often than you are used to. While this gives you the reassurance you need to move ahead with plans, don't forget to listen to your inner voice. Your instincts are good and if you have a feeling something is not right, it probably isn't. While others may try to give you an unbiased outside perspective of your situation, no one can make better decisions than you. You may have to turn down some good opportunities that are hard to resist, but if the risks are too high, it is not worth taking them. Other opportunities will come again, but for now, lying low is your safest bet. There are no shortcuts to success, and this will quickly become clear this month.

Love & Relationships - *Keep your spirits up*

Staying put and being where you are right now is better than trying to take your relationship to the next level. Be happy nothing is going wrong with your love life. If you have been allowing certain hang-ups to worry you, now is the time to get rid of them. These worrisome thoughts can only hamper what can be a loving relationship between you. Be supportive of your partner who may be going through a worse time than you. The more upbeat you are, the better. Your positive mood can be infectious and when you smile, the world laughs with you. Your mood will rub off on your partner so you should maintain a cheerful disposition even if things are dragging you down.

Home & Family - *Rivalry*

There are differing opinions on the home front and some arguments may occur among siblings. If you are involved in sibling rivalry, check your pros and cons to see if you should stand your ground or give in, since blood is still thicker than water.

Education - *Specialise*

It is better to do a few things really well and receive all the kudos than to do many things poorly. Otherwise, people you wish to impress may remember you for a mediocre job!

CURE FOR THE MONTH: Carry the **Five Element Pagoda with Tree of Life Amulet** this month to dispel the negative effects of the Five Yellow.

6th Month
July 7th - Aug 7th 2021

STRONG LUCK BRINGS JOY & SUCCESS

Your luck is strong this month, especially when it comes to commercial ventures. Exciting opportunities to make money come your way and those who put your minds to it can significantly increase your net worth. Career luck gets a boost and you may well get that promotion you have been hankering for. Business worries recede and things fall nicely into place. A month when you feel like a weight is lifting off your shoulders. Obstacles magically disappear, making you wonder why you worried so much in the first place. Enjoy yourself and don't be so uptight. The more relaxed you are, the better your judgement. Does not mean you take a holiday and do not lift a finger, but stop worrying about every little thing that can go wrong and instead, focus on the positives.

Work & Career - *Expanding your influence*

Things look very optimistic at work. A month to start broadening your horizons. You find new ways to contribute and begin to feel an integral part of the team, no longer the outsider with quirky ideas. Others value your contribution and the more conviction you have in your own work, the more others value your input. You may be approached frequently for your opinion on matters that may not usually involve you. While you hesitate to tread on someone else's turf, as long as you remain mindful, your response will be appreciated.

A good time to grow your position in your job. Keep putting in the effort. You can make big strides this month.

Business - *Big ideas*

Dragons in business benefit from having crystal clear objectives. Develop a strategy but don't let yourself get slowed down by worrying about details. Have your main ideas firmly in place first and the rest will follow. You are fuelled with the kind of passion that can turn your ideas into spectacular and noteworthy results. Ventures started now have every chance of success, so when good opportunities present themselves, make the best of them. You enjoy excellent rapport with those you work with; develop this further. When you have to place trust in somebody, go with a known quantity. A time to build on what is good. You can dabble in new things as well, but don't let it dilute your focus. Be progressive in your thinking and press all the forward buttons in your life.

Love & Relationships - *Be bold!*

Love is in the air! If you have been secretly admiring someone, now is the best time to let your feelings known. Fortune favours the bold and very much so in your case right now. Others find you attractive so just be yourself. There is no need to put on airs. You have what it takes and there is no justification in trying to be something else. If looking to get hitched, you do so in the blink of an eye. Those married will find your spouses great sources of support and affection. Enjoy the month!

Home & Family - *Connecting well*

Family vacations are guaranteed big successes, so if you have the time and money, take the family for a holiday and you will create great memories to last for years. If pressed for time, organize reunion dinners and get-togethers. Quality time spent with family augurs well.

Education - *Specialise*

Your stars shine bright and you are in line to win scholarships and honours. Now is the time to prove you have what it takes. There is nothing too tough for you. As long as you are sufficiently prepared, you do very well indeed!

ENHANCER FOR THE MONTH: Carry the **Windhorse Success Amulet** to boost good fortune luck; wear **Yellow Dzambala's Prayer Wheel Pendant** for wealth.

7th Month
Aug 8th - Sept 7th 2021

DIFFICULT MONTH WHEN ROBBERY STAR SOURS THE ENERGY

Not a great month since there are dangers from robbery and you may get betrayed, cheated or let down, financially or emotionally. Certain bad things make you feel life is treating you unfairly, but you must see all the goodies it has given you last month. The trials and tribulations now are not to be compared with the excessive treasures of your good months. When the going gets tough, take a step back and enjoy the little things you took for granted when the going was good. Strike a balance between work and play; once you get this equation right, you will be much happier and more pleasant. By extension, you will also perform better in the workplace when not so obsessed with the finishing line!

Work & Career - *Workplace politics*

Things are not as smooth as you would like. Some colleagues simply relish upsetting you, but keep your chin up. By appearing non-plussed, you are beating them at their own game. There may be nasty politicking going on but console yourself this happens everywhere; you are not the first nor the last to bear the brunt of idle gossip.

An overly competitive environment can drain your energy; sometimes it seems there is one too many in your cubicle. You wish to concentrate but it is not easy with so many distractions. You are expected to deliver on time, within budget and eagle eyes are on you. If you slip up now, the world will notice! Maintain your regular work pace; don't let anyone push you lest you make careless mistakes. Don't expect rewards now and brace yourself for criticism. Accolades will come later.

Don't trust others easily. Rely on your own judgement. If in doubt, avoid, refrain, restrain and retreat!

Business - *Trust your own instincts*

There may be disputes over money matters as you discover some glaring discrepancies. It gets worse if it involves one or more partners as everyone passes the buck and ducks the blame. Even before the clouds clear, other partners may not see eye-to-eye with you. Problems are exacerbated if a third party enters the picture! Your own decisions are more valuable than checking with others who may have their own hidden agenda. They may give bad advice, or worse, trick you with false data. Brainstorming is not worth the time spent, so stick to your own guns. Continue doing what you are good at. Ignore snide remarks. Wealth luck is weak, so you already stand to lose a large chunk, so don't take any more risks.

Love & Relationships - *More care needed*

There may be trouble brewing on the love front. Arguments and misunderstandings stem from mistrust, so work on building up trust. Don't get influenced by others against your own partner. If you want your relationship to work, you need to be more protective of your relationship than you currently are. Stand up for each other instead of allowing an outsider influence how you feel. Those happily married need to watch for troublemakers. Don't succumb to the charms of third parties, and don't drive your partner into the arms of somebody else by being inattentive or distracted.

Education - *Take breaks*

Luck is only moderate this month, but you can overcome lethargy and low concentration levels by taking breaks every now and then. Don't try to put in more hours if your mind is tired. Better to take a break with a favourite hobby, sport or even TV. You need a refreshed mind to be effective.

CURE FOR THE MONTH: Dragons in business need the **Kuan Kung on Horseback Anti-Betrayal Amulet** this month. Lady Dragons who go out late at night should carry the **Nightspot Protection Amulet**.

8th Month
Sept 8th - Oct 7th 2021

LUCK FALLS FROM THE HEAVENS!

So many delightful and beneficial things to look forward to! After the frustrations and irritations of last month, you are all set to enjoy a period of peace, progress and prosperity! Opportunities abound where you can demonstrate your talents, help those in need and make money. Now is the time to think also about charity work since money seems to come easily. The more you give, the happier you feel. You have many interesting options but can't have them all, so decide which appeal to you most and then go for them! Chances are high you succeed quite gloriously! You also enjoy mentor luck; someone in a position to help you enters your life and takes an interest in you. Cultivate such relationships.

Work & Career - *Rethinking things*

Developing good relationships with superiors stands you in good stead and helps you leapfrog to the next level, so actively cultivate such friendships. If you feel less than satisfied, re-look your career and weigh your options. Calculate your goals and see if they are achievable in your current company and position. You may have a surprising rethink of ideas and what seems outrageous may seem attractive and vice versa. You are in line to meet a mentor who will play an important role. Even if they do not contribute financially, their indirect influence will have a great bearing on your immediate future.

You have the kind of luck this month that causes everything to fall into place exactly as it should, so take confidence in that.

Business - *Talented negotiator*

Brainstorming works better than trying to figure everything out on your own. Meetings and even casual discussions are productive and can generate some really great ideas. Plans put into motion may not bring instant riches but will add to your company's revenues in the medium term, so patience is a virtue here. Not only is your wealth luck good but you also experience some form of windfall.

You are feeling confident and composed, which puts you at ease in most situations. This makes this an ideal time to enter into new deals or negotiate new terms with those you do business with. You hold all the aces, but also possess incredible charm, which makes others feel they are benefitting from whatever you are proposing. You have the knack of pitching everything just right, and those of you bidding for contracts and concessions have a good chance of being successful.

Love & Relationships - *Don't play games*

Romantic matters boost your self-esteem. Those single and looking have every chance to find someone special this month. Some of you may be spoilt for choice, but don't let yourself go down a road where you concoct up a love triangle. This will lead to emotions you cannot handle. Don't play games when it comes to the heart, because yours is more fragile than you think. You could ruin a perfectly good chance to have something long-lasting with someone very special.

Home & Family - *Precious advice*

Devote more time to elderly members of your family; one may be particularly drawn towards you for some inexplicable reason. Do not let this person down. Take advice when you know it is given in good faith. There may be more to it than meets the eye. Mentor luck is strong and some older member of the family can give advice that is more precious than you realise now. Listen up.

Education - *Mentor luck*

You enjoy mentor luck and find someone who takes you under their wing. They open your eyes to a much clearer future and could help you to make up your mind in some important decisions that will arise in your life shortly.

ENHANCER FOR THE MONTH: Carry the **Dragon Heavenly Seal Amulet** to boost the *Heaven Star* in your chart this month.

9th Month
Oct 8th - Nov 6th 2021

SUM-OF-TEN
BUT BEWARE FIVE YELLOW

A difficult month when the *wu wang* in your chart gets doubled. When the Five Yellow strikes, the advice is to take things slow, consider your every move, refrain from impulsive reactions. It is absolutely necessary to suppress the ill effects of the Five Yellow with the right cures, the best being the Five Element Pagoda. Clip a portable one onto your bag so you always have one near you. But there is a silver lining! When the wu wang doubles, it also creates the very lucky *sum-of-ten* configuration, which brings you good fortune and completion luck. The coming month is a mixed one where obstacles are mixed up with opportunities. Sort the wheat from the chaff and the next four weeks could bring some exciting prospects!

Work & Career - *Work quietly*

Keep an eagle eye on your work as mistakes are easily made. Most can be corrected before anyone notices so the ball is in your court not to be careless. Avoid sweeping dust under the carpet as you will be found out. Don't break company rules even if you think they are minor. Once you start, it becomes a habit that gets hard to stop. If you feel your employer is unappreciative, put it down to misconception and don't get petty. Work diligently and quietly. Try not to stand out too much. Better to be viewed as a stalwart member of the team who is always dependable than a wannabe superstar. Your personal luck cannot handle this right now, so keep a low profile.

If you are ambitious, keep your ambitions to yourself. Letting everyone know how eager you are to reach the top will do you no good at all.

Business - *Don't lose heart*

There are opportunities to generate sales or make additional revenues but somehow you just keep missing them! You either hear the news too late or lose out through some technical hitch. All this upsets your morale and your staff seem lackluster as well. Try as you might, these pockets of income keep slipping through your fingers and a miss is as good as a mile. Don't lose heart and more importantly, don't lose more money. Avoid short term investments that promise fast returns. Don't take risks and rein in expenses. Take some initiatives of your own provided they do not entail costly expenditures, but do not expect too much too quickly. Think long term when making investment plans.

Love & Relationships - *Misunderstandings*

Not the most harmonious of times when it comes to love and relationships. Misunderstandings loom ahead. Be the bigger person in difficult situations or you could end up with a big fight on your hands. Those in stable relationships should watch you don't lose what you have from your quick temper. Walk away from an argument if you have to. Better to give yourself time to cool off than say things you regret later.

Home & Family - *Mediator*

Your family and relatives hardly rise to the occasion nor offer much solace or comfort. In fact, you find them irritating and they are not enamoured by you either! Even with your children, you may have some misunderstandings. If there are rifts between relatives, you may be forced to be mediator. You feel you are in no position to negotiate but in your haste to extricate yourself, make sure you don't accidentally add fuel to the fire!

Education - *No winging it*

For the young Dragon, this is a month when you can make a big impression. There is success luck to be tapped but you need to tap it right. While you have plenty of natural talent and charisma, these alone won't clinch you that scholarship or job offer. But back that up with hard work, preparation and research and you can unlock many incredible opportunities this month. Do your homework, don't show up for anything unprepared, and the month is yours.

10th Month
Nov 7th - Dec 6th 2021

RELATIONSHIPS MATTER

Joy this month comes from success in relationships, particularly romantic ones. It will be far easier to gain ground when it comes to influencing the decisions of those around you. Friends are attentive and you find their support invaluable. Socially, you are in your element and your talent for getting along with others stands you in good stead to make significant advances whether in work, business or personal matters. Be prepared to spend time and effort cultivating your friendships, but this does not mean you shouldn't be discerning. Have a strategy when building up allies, particularly when it comes to business associates. There is also good study luck for the young Dragon and those taking exams fare well.

Work & Career - *Working well with others*

You make good progress at work. Use the month to build up friendships with those you work with. Your colleagues are particularly responsive to your suggestions. You are filled with many ideas concerning work and implementing them to your company's benefit seems easy. You have a newfound confidence that can be put to good use at the workplace. Use your leadership qualities to start new initiatives. You are a natural people person to begin with, and now that you are allowed to be in your element, you can really blossom to everyone's advantage.

Working in a team or by yourself will be beneficial, but avoid working with just one other person of the opposite sex too closely. If you find you become involved in a project where just you and one other person have to constantly stay late at the office together, find a way to extricate yourself in a suitable fashion.

Business - *Networking luck*

Your strength this month comes from getting along with others. You have the ability to crack jokes at just the right moment and you gauge your audience well. A good time to strike new deals, impress those you need to impress, and to network aggressively. You pitch new ideas well and give convincing presentations. Those working in research make some exciting breakthroughs.

You are in a good position to get what you want if you stay organized. Put your networking skills to good use by actively mixing with others. Mingling with the competition may trigger new ideas that prove useful. Financial luck is good and there are opportunities to profit from. Don't just roll along with a mundane routine; be bold if you want to make definite progress.

Love & Relationships - *Love grows*

Relationships started now have a high chance of
success. There are different possibilities suggesting
themselves. Pick one to develop into something more
than just friendship; something special can grow from
that. Use your imagination for ideas to romance your
mate. When it comes to love, nothing is too crazy. Make
the most of this time to fall head over heels. As long as
your personal life is not interfering with work, it can
only enrich your life. Just be sure to maintain a balance
by not overdoing things!

Home & Family - *Make time*

You feel attached to your family but due to
circumstances beyond your control, you tend to be
away more than you like - whether on company trips or
having to work late. Spend quality time with the family
when you can; you derive happiness doing the most
ordinary things with them. Involve the whole family in
group activities or short vacations away.

Education - *Scholastic luck*

A fabulous month for the student Dragon. You have
scholarly luck on your side, so those taking exams
benefit. Creativity comes in different guises. Adopt
whatever study method you prefer; whether your
inspiration comes in short flashes of brilliance, or
manifests after hours of steady study, the results will
be handsome. Keep up the motivation and watch as the
results roll in!

11th Month
Dec 7th - Jan 5th 2022

ARGUMENTS ABOUND. BEWARE.

The quarrelsome star brings arguments and misunderstandings. Avoid getting into situations of conflict. Small issues have the tendency to work themselves into bigger ones if not kept in check. You could face problems with the law and authorities if not careful. Not a good time to deal with anything official. If you can help it, don't put anything down on paper. Avoid signing deals and agreements. Entering into partnerships could lead to problems surfacing after. Rely on yourself when making important decisions. Do not get others involved because it will be difficult to distinguish who has your best interests at heart. Lie low when it comes to important things. A good time to get away and simply take a vacation.

Work & Career - *Challenging*

Not only is work challenging but fraught with delays unless you rein in your temper and be less argumentative. You tend to alienate others and force them to retreat, taking along their goodwill that can facilitate your tasks. Instead of criticizing others, why not admit your mistake? Best to work relatively alone and only collaborate with others when you need. Too much interacting becomes counterproductive and relationships could sour. Do not let your emotions get the better of you when dealing with work rivals. As long as you keep your attitude in check, and act with your head and not your heart, you can come out the winner.

Business - *Technical hitches*

You are confronted with technical hitches, human errors are bureaucratic red tape, so your nerves are on edge. It is even worse should you take your grouses to a higher authority, as they are even less sympathetic. Better to grit your teeth and carry on till you see the light at the end of the tunnel. Not a good time for new partnerships. Success rates are low. Instead, focus on your human resources. There may be some instances of fighting among your staff, which can lead to stalled work and lowered productivity. You have to intervene, mediate and if necessary, perform drastic surgery by deciding who has to go.

You may find those in authority making life difficult for you. Do not risk being penalized for no reason. If there are licenses or permits you need to have, be sure you apply well in advance.

Love & Relationships - *Quarrelsome*
There is plenty of quarrelsome energy in the air, so anyone you are with will seem more disagreeable than usual. Do not be surprised if you and your partner are at each other's throats much of the time. As long as your arguments don't turn into cold wars, things work out. Try not to be too serious. If a discussion gets too heated or starts to touch on sensitive topics, laugh off your differences if you want to make your relationship work.

Education - *Competitive*
The young Dragon needs to watch the company you keep. You could fall under bad influence and be led astray. Don't let yourself be talked into doing things you wouldn't usually do. This is an easy time to get into trouble if you break the rules.

CURE FOR THE MONTH: Carry the **Apple Peace Amulet** to smooth over the conflict energies of the month. Place the **28 Hums Protection Wheel** with **Heart Sutra** on your desk, so you don't attract the wrath of those envious of you, or who are angry for some reason or another.

28 Hums Protection
Wheel with Heart Sutra

12th Month
Jan 6th - Feb 3rd 2022

ILLNESS STAR
IMPACTS ON YOUR ENERGY LEVELS

The illness star affects your health, saps your energy and brings risk of accidents and mishaps. When it combines with the Five Yellow like it does now, its strength gets magnified, making it even more important for you not to take warning signs lightly. Small ailments could become more serious if not looked after. Don't push yourself too hard. If you need a rest, take a break. Don't try to do everything yourself. Avoid indulging in risky sports. When driving, don't drive too fast and definitely you must not drink and drive. Travel is not favoured so if you must travel, carry amulets. Lead a healthy lifestyle and even if you end up in a pensive mood, it is better than getting sick or being involved in an accident!

Work & Career - *Work smart*

Work smart rather than hard since your body is showing its limits. Develop or maintain close ties with those whose paths you cross daily, as you need their help and support. Success comes from getting along with workmates whose cooperation you need. This is not a time to be overly ambitious as whatever you do may not lead anywhere, so it may be a waste of time and effort when you should be looking at the small picture instead. Completing your daily tasks is more rewarding than trying to impress. Trying to please everyone is not feasible now and if you fail, your superiors may not be that understanding.

Don't take on hefty assignments you cannot realistically handle; a costly mistake now can seriously affect your career.

Business - *Avoid risk-taking*

Be careful when embarking on new pursuits and strategies. Your financial luck is poor, so avoid taking risks. Watch your cash flow more closely and do not incur unnecessary expenditure; this is a time to conserve. You may have more frequent interaction with other industry players; this is a good thing as you have much to learn from those in similar businesses as you. While some may be your rivals, others could end up becoming synergistic partners. You're not feeling your best in terms of health, so even small tasks could seem major. Make time for a break to clear your mind when needed; even a little time off can make all the difference. Learn to trust other people, especially when it is your own people. Don't try to do everything yourself. The larger your goals, the more control you have to concede. Manage more effectively so you can scale your operations and not have to do everything yourself. If your health is telling you to slow down, listen.

Love & Relationships - *Changing values*

Every aspect of your life is full up, leaving you little time to devote to building relationships, and even less time to dedicate to your love life. Not the best of times if hoping to find a life partner in the conventional way; instead, you could find yourself falling for someone you never thought you had any romantic inclinations for. Your values could be changing. Don't limit your horizons by what you think others expect of you. Go with the flow and happiness will be easier to achieve.

Health - *Under the weather*

Look after your health. Your defenses are down and you're more likely to catch viruses and succumb to falling sick. If you don't feel well, don't brush it aside. Let someone know before it gets worse. Sleep matters, so get enough.

Education - *Don't try to be too perfect*

You may not be feeling on top of your game. Start your assignments early so you do not end up panicking when racing against deadlines. Don't try to be too much of a perfectionist, just get things done.

CURE FOR THE MONTH: Carry the **Wu Lou Health Amulet** to keep illness energies at bay. Those who need to travel should wear protective amulets.